RESURGIUS

a sex comedy

RESURGIUS

a sex comedy

E.M. SCHORB

HILL HOUSE   NEW YORK

ISBN: 979-8-218-43121-1

Cover Design: Selah Bunzey

Cover Portrait: "Serge" by E.M. Schorb

ACKNOWLEDGEMENTS

The poems "The Naked Truth" first appeared in *The Lyric* magazine, "O Popular Moon" in *Bitterroot International Poetry Journal,* and "From the Esplanade" in *The Hudson Review.*

. . . to see one-half of the human race excluded by the other from all participation in government was a political phenomenon that, according to abstract principles, it was impossible to explain.

*   *   *

I do not wish women to have power over men; but over themselves.

A Vindication of the Rights of Woman
—Mary Wollstonecraft

<u>1</u>

To Serge Bering-Strait, young ward of five aggressive, progressive, and, to him, oppressive, women, the phrase "Swinging Sixties," meant, at this moment, swinging like Tarzan from a subway strap.

But he was no Tarzan. His mother and four aunties had forced *him*, a *poet*, out of his Greenwich Village attic sanctuary and into the struggle for survival here among the *poloi,* where he felt in imminent danger of being crushed, which partly accounted for the look of angst he wore. But what really depressed Serge was that he had already missed a whole half-hour of reading from his beloved Plutarch's *Parallel Lives*, which he gripped under his free arm, and which was being pressed painfully into his ribs by a grubby fellow traveler. The "lumpen mob" was just too thick this morning, too thick to hold up his book—so thick, in fact, that he was not sure if he had missed his stop.

There were no signs in prominent display, the windows were painted gaily over with spray paint, and the terrific, ear-splitting cough made by the loud-speaker hadn't served in the least to clear things up. Serge decided to get out.

The train doors shut just as he stepped through them, smudging the shoulders of his new London Fog, a twenty-third birthday gift from his Auntie Janet Hoover, and knocking his copy of Plutarch's *Lives* from his grasp. The book was kicked ahead of him into obscurity by the mob's stampeding hooves. The train re-opened its doors with a snort, shot them shut behind him, and pulled away.

It was the wrong station. Well, it was a natural enough mistake. He had not had time to develop that sixth sense about subway stops that comes with practice. He had only been on the job for a few weeks, his Auntie Janet Hoover having procured his position as staff writer for him through her connection with the boss, the lady editor Bettina Battle, who sometimes worked for Auntie Hoover as a speech writer. Auntie Hoover was in politics, an assistant to Mayor Dimwiddy.

This was not his first job. His first job was being a poet, which he had been since his prodigious graduation from New York University some five years before, at eighteen. But Auntie Hoover thought that it was high time that the little "genius-boy" got out of the house. She thought his life up in his garret room was very unnatural.

When the crowd thinned, Serge found his battered Plutarch near the turnstile. He could have cried for the thousand indifferent kicks it had received. A tasteless modern world had no respect for the classics.

A train roared in, with a long, shrill, metallic scream of the sort he imagined Jurassic raptors might have used to indicate their ravenousness.

Pressed into the center of the crushed subway crowd, which held him upright, levitated, feet adrift in space, arms bound to his sides, his Plutarch bruising his ribs, he could still get a sniff of fetid hot air from above; but the air-conditioning blew his inherently wild red hair askew and, when he opened his spectacled eyes, he was forced to look at the advertising signs over the windows. HEMORRHOIDS?

one asked, distastefully. TAMPONS? another invited. UNDERARM ODOR? another challenged. JOCK ITCH! another asserted. THE NAKED TRUTH another—wait!

THE NAKED TRUTH?

Ah ha! The bureaucrats at the Poetry in Motion office had finally got around to putting up his subway poem—

THE NAKED TRUTH

The naked truth will lie.
I don't believe in facts.
What's in the inner eye
Is what the outer lacks.

The night's an Arab's sheet
Of swirling blue and black.
The earth is at his feet.
The stars are at his back.

And even love is true
If we should make it so.
O, lover, love me too!
O, lover, let me go!

by Serge Bering- . . .

The lights in the car flickered, went out. Serge thought of his loss of time. It seemed hours till they got started again, but it turned out to be only twelve minutes when he could read his watch.

The light turned green in Serge's favor and he stepped out from the curb, preoccupied with thoughts of his dreary, poetry-corrupting writing job, his guilty tardiness, when a taxi swerved in front of him with a screech, blasting its horn, the driver, a woman who looked as mean as Auntie Hoover, cursing him with words even more raffish than passages from Allen Ginsburg's horrible "Howl." As his eyes rolled back in his head, Mother Nature's eternal blue highway shone between the tall, artificial escarpments of skyscrapers, still, surprisingly, possessing the magic of modernity—and he saw, high above him, in that blue wonder, an airship shaped like a Frankfurter. It was the Quaint Wiener Balloon, the inescapable red hot dog that he saw in every store, at every stand; but this one was gigantic, so big that it out-loomed the skyscrapers, seemed to even outloom the Goodyear *dirigible*!

QUAINT WIENERS

was written on its side, plain as day. And then, it floated out of sight, banned from the sky by the behemoth buildings it sailed over.

He entered the revolving door of the American Rubber Climax Building and was shot up sixty-nine floors to the offices of *Women's Omnibus* magazine. He got to work just on time but was immediately assaulted.

"Your 'food-on-a-stick' article is très—and I do mean *très*—putrid," cried Serge's editor, Bettina Battle, sometimes known as the Battle of Britain, having arrived at *Women's Omnibus* from *Swinging London*, the magazine as well as the city.

"What's wrong with it?" Serge was shaking out his London Fog. He hung it on the clothes tree that took up valuable foot space in his cubicle. It was a sad, dripping sight. His Auntie Janet would sting with the insult of it. But then, Auntie Janet Hoover was always prepared to sting. He wiped his face and dried his glasses with tissue, superficially listening to Bettina Battle's cockney-inclined locutions while inwardly bemoaning the condition of his battered Plutarch. He had to pee.

"What's wrong with it?" Bettina Battle cried. "That's old shit! We want something new! We want new concepts! On the ball, Bering-Strait! On the ball!"

Serge could scarcely keep his eyes open. He'd been awake since two a.m. when the burglar alarm went off at Schlock's Delicatessen down the street from his mother's house. Since his air conditioner was on the blink, and his window wide open, he'd heard the alarm full blast. "New concepts," he ruminated. "Food-on-a-stick, just heat and eat."

"What's that?" cried Bettina Battle.

"What do you mean 'new concepts'?" asked Serge. "The stuff's a lot of dreck. Who'd eat it?"

"Bering-Strait, what are you saying?"

The din of electric Selectric typewriters and office machines seemed particularly intense. His head ached, and he had to pee, badly. He took a bottle of aspirins from his desk and walked to the water cooler with Bettina Battle in pestering pursuit. She eyed him ruefully as he choked down two aspirins.

"This is serious business, Bering-Strait," she said, while he strangled on the aspirins, repeatedly flushing them down with paper cup after paper cup of water. It was business, Serge admitted to himself, and the money involved made it serious, he supposed; but it was disgusting, nonetheless. He yearned for the classics. He even yearned for Jane Austen. If only Bettina Battle spoke to him like a character out of Jane Austen instead of sounding like the screeching flower girl in "My Fair Lady."

"You see, Bering-Strait, the mashed potatoes, ground beef, and peas are all smooshed up together into a ball, like a lollipop, and frozen on a stick. Then you pop it in the oven, and there it is, ready to eat! A quick meal for busy women in a busy women's world." Bettina beamed. "Isn't it wonderful? It's a new concept!" Now Bettina frowned.

"You've got to get serious, Bering-Strait. Magazines are in stiff competition with—I can hardly bear to say it—the telly, TV, the tube, say-screen, or whatever you want to call that monster."

"Say-screen?"

"Whatever—call the monster what you will—it's ruining our circulation. That's why we need new concepts."

"Won't it fall off when it's heated?"

"Won't what fall off?"

"The food off the stick! Won't it fall off when it's heated?"

Bettina looked at him, hard. "Uuum. You look beat, Bering-Strait. What's the matter, not getting enough sleep?"

"No, I'm *not* getting enough sleep," Serge said, yawning, "I was up all night. First a faulty alarm went off and woke me and my air conditioner's on the blink, and then I couldn't stop thinking about a novel I want to write."

"Novels are dead! Flicks and the Say-screen have already killed them. Do you want the monster to kill *Women's Omnibus* as well? Here, we need people who can think on their feet around here—think original thoughts, new concepts," Bettina summed up. She stood looking at him, arms akimbo, waiting like a drill sergeant for a response from a recruit.

"Something like Amanda Quaint's idea

for sky-mirrors?" Serge asked insinuatingly. Amanda Quaint wrote for a competitor of *Women's Omnibus, Ladies' Day*, and her recent article had caused a great stir among the New York magazine set. Leo Lerman had called her a genius.

"Quite, Bering-Strait, that's quite it! Think of it—constant daylight—'round the clock selling! Business would double. The world would have to run three shifts. Then too, it'd create a whole new market—sleeping aids; ear-plugs; sleeping pills; eye shades; black window curtains! Think of that, Bering-Strait! New concepts! By the way, I want you to get started on researching the new UNIVAC machine."

"The great computer that's going to revolutionize life as we know it?"

"I want the angle on what it'll do for women—help free them from low-paying office drudgery—"

Serge saw himself in his cubicle, wetting his pants.

"—elevate them to technical personnel, programmers and the like. See what you can bring out of the tin. I want some stats on women—proving their oppression. Up till now we've only had deductive reasoning to go by—observation. Now, with this UNIVAC III, we can get statistics to prove scientifically what we've believed all along, that we women are nothing but drudges and slaves for you men. The UNIVAC III will set women free!"

Serge asked, "Won't it just increase production, rather than freeing any workers?"

Bettina didn't approve of Serge's obvious lack of enthusiasm. "I've got my eye on you, Bering-Strait." She turned and marched off on stiletto heels.

Serge could not run to the lavatory, for fear of losing urinary control, but he got there as soon as he could. All the urinals were vacant, but Serge was urinal-averse. He went into a booth, sat down, and peed. His mother and aunties had trained him from a toddler to sit down when he peed in order to reduce splashing and mistargeting, or so they told him, taught him, and now it was impossible for him to stand and shoot. He washed his hands and went back to the office.

Serge spent most of the afternoon acquainting himself with his new assignment. He'd have to figure out the female angle on the Univac III. What would it mean to readers of *Women's Omnibus*?

At four-thirty, Serge begged to be unhanded by Bettina, who dragged him from his cubicle—where he had been racking his brains—and into her glassed-in corner office.

"Sir Gay . . ." she began, lighting a Virginia Slim, sinking into her swivel chair, and putting her amazingly long and shapely legs on her desk, spike-heels spindling articles that covered every aspect of women's life from hair-dos to toenail polish, from gourmet cooking to commodity investments ("How Women Can Make a Million in Pork Bellies").

"Serge!" he corrected. "Why do you always call me Sir Gay? You know that my name is pronounced 'surge' like the surge of the sea."

"Whatsum," Bettina said. "Thing is, I've had my eye on you for some time."

"So you said," said Serge, with a snip in his voice.

"You're a presentable young man in a poufy sort of way, and I'd like you to escort me to a meeting of the Lunar Society in Greenwich Village tonight. *I* live in the Village and *you* live in the Village, so, after the meeting, you can see me home . . . or should I see *you* home? It'll be getting dark by then. I have a black belt in Karate, so you have no need to fear the mean streets of the Village after sundown."

Serge understood her sarcasm. The infamous nymphomaniac had been trying to get into his virginal pants since his first day on the job, but he had thus far managed to fend her off. She had gone from merely chiding him to outright bitchy persecution. Clearly, however, she was going to have another try tonight, taking a different tack. It was not that her beauty did not appeal to him, but that she had none of the sweetness his embarrassed virginity would require in his first lover. Her beauty was controlled by a harsh machine, a soulless battery, that energized a force field. In other words, she turned him off, but good!

"What's the Lunar Society?" he asked, trying to show polite interest.

"The Lunar Society is an association of professional women who meet monthly, and I am surprised, your mother and aunties being who they are, that you have not heard of it. *Our Mother is the Moon!* Doesn't that ring a bell?"

It did, faintly. A tiny tinkle. But, for as long as he could remember, he had been dragged to all sorts of meetings, conventions, and gatherings, yet, somehow, had managed, maybe, to have missed this particular one; or perhaps had actually slept through an earlier meeting of the Lunar Society, as he often slept through meetings, even sometimes snored through them. Sometimes all he had to show for a meeting was a bruised rib cage, where female elbows had poked him awake. His ribs were tender as a bird's.

"Why me?" he asked. "You can get anybody you want to escort you." But he already knew the answer. She wanted something new. Even a new disease would do for Bettina.

"Why must we go?" he asked.

"Because everyone who's anyone in the Women's Movement will be there. Don't you want to get somewhere in the magazine business? Well, you have to be inside. It's called networking. Besides, your whole family will be there. Now, no buts about it. Meet me at my limo out in front at five-thirty sharp. I have no more bloody time to spend on you. Not now. But I have something of great importance to tell you on the drive downtown." She pointed a long, ensanguined talon toward his cubicle, over the bobbing heads of busy, quietly desperate plebes. "Go!" she ordered, and closed the valves of her attention, as Emily Dickinson might have done.

At five-thirty sharp, Serge stood, like a reactionary lemming, a few feet in front of the revolving art deco door of the American Rubber Climax Building and refused to be moved by the outflowing crowd. Curiosity kept him in place. What was this thing of "great importance" that Bettina had waved before him like a carrot? And could he avoid the stick?

In the limo, a breathless Bettina Battle told him that she would be leaving *Women's Omnibus* poste-haste, for a better job, and that he might very well be her replacement as editor of the magazine. Her contract allowed her final choice for the editorship and her eye was on him, she said. "Yes, my eye is on *you*," she repeated, squeezing his thigh.

He giggled, squirming. Her thumb had plucked a funny string in his leg.

"Gawd!" she exclaimed. "You're so skinny. I hope there is something a bit more hefty in that region. Shall we see?" She reached out again, her fingers dancing like red-tipped spider legs.

"Yipes!"

To Serge, her offer of promotion seemed far-fetched, but curiosity kept him listening, as well as patiently struggling, almost arm-wrestling. But there was this little problem, eh? And so began a battle for Serge's honor in the back seat of Bettina Battle's limousine. His red suspenders were no match for her black belt. Putting a purr in her otherwise harsh voice, she whispered, "I hate these big macho muscle men. It's you cute little cuddly guys like Woody Allen I go for in a big way. You remind me of him."

She twirled his red and white polka-dot bow tie, and lifted her short skirt up to her creamy hip to show that she wore no knickers. There was a growling British lion tattooed on her hip with some writing under it. She started to lower the skirt but Serge stopped her.

"Wait!" he said. "What's that say?" And then he was able to read the legend: I'LL EAT YOU ALIVE.

"Good heavens!" Serge cried. He was appalled. He felt that any kind of tattoo or body-piercing was primitive, déclassé; simultaneously transfixing and stomach-turning.

"Hurry the bloody hell up," she cried, releasing her skirt to the grip of gravity. "It's a long dull drive downtown. Let's ball, baby!"

Her focus on the mechanics of unjamming his zipper had caused her not to realize that they had already arrived at the Village home of Hettie Freed, renowned author of *Men: The Feminine Mistake.*

Before Bettina could find a way to get his pants down, she found it necessary to make herself presentable. As she dabbed at her makeup, she said, "I never wear knickers, myself. I'm like the Boy Scouts—always prepared. I strongly suggest you heed my example next time. Get a pair of pants with buttons that button up. I can bite off a button."

She was miffed, but it wasn't his fault that she couldn't get his pants down, except for the struggling induced by his animal instinct for survival. He pulled his zipper up, then down, then up again, and it was free, and so was he. Silently, he thanked the jammed zipper heartily for protecting his terrified pee-pee, which seemed to shrink an inch back into his body at every touch of her long red talons. He pulled up his off-the-shoulder suspenders, got back into the jacket and London Fog she had fairly ripped from his back, stuck his Plutarch under his arm, and followed the Amazonian Bettina like a small, neurotic mutt on an umbilical leash.

The words "Hurry up, *Sir Gay!*" wafted over her shoulder on an ill wind, seeming to come from her tall French twist, as she climbed the steps of Hettie Freed's brownstone on Horatio Street, toward the networking delights of the Lunar Society's monthly meeting.

"My name is Serge, sounds like a *surge* of the sea!" he called after Bettina Battle, but she was not listening. The door swung open and she feinted a kiss on each dangling jowl of Hettie Freed, who asked who her little companion was. "This is Sir Gay Bering-Strait. You probably know his mother, Dagmar Bering-Strait—"

"—who invented bra-burning? Yes, of course I know Dagmar. She's here. I'm surprised I haven't met Sir Gay before this."

"My name is Serge. Like the *surge* of the sea," he insisted.

"*Gay* is quite an imaginative writer," said Bettina Battle. "He just finished a wonderful piece for *Women's Omnibus* on food-on-a-stick, and is even now researching the new UNIVAC III machine for an article on its impact on the lives of women. He is a gifted journalist, so gifted that he should never do anything else, and I'm quite sure he has no thought of changing to another line of work. He says he wants to write a novel, though. Am I right, Gay?"

Serge nodded in defeat.

"Sounds brilliant, darling!" said Hettie, patting Serge on the head. Out of politeness, he tried to wag his tail a bit.

"And you know who else is here tonight?" Hettie's grey jowls brightened with the blood of excitement. "That delightful new discovery who wrote the piece in your competitor's magazine about sky-mirrors—you know, so that no one can sleep. Oh, what is she called?"

"Amanda Quaint—yes," said Bettina, "I'm anxious to meet her."

Had Serge's mother introduced him to Hettie Freed, he'd have become the subject of a dissertation. Dagmar would have regaled Hettie with her favorite explanation for Serge's existence. "He was conceived," his mother would have claimed, "in a public swimming pool, and is the ward of the State of New York. Floating semen, you see. . ." And she would have gone into the long legal battle she had with the State.

The truth was that his father, Charles Bering-Strait, was dead, having died in a wine-soaked cardboard box behind the Port Authority Bus Terminal. His mother had rid herself of the "loathsome sex maniac" at an early stage of their marriage. Serge had once read a letter from his father to his mother that bore the salutation "Dear Furious," so he had some ideas of his own about their marriage.

He was certain that he had been named by his mother, not his father. He thought of the torment of his school days. Even the progressive schools that she had sent him to were torture chambers if you bore such a name as "Serge" and had been taught to sit down like a girl when you peed.

He followed Bettina Battle and Hettie Freed into the cavernous living room, acquired a glass of Dom Pérignon with little stars rising in it, and took two of the "Rosebud" wafers topped with darling little pink vaginas—someone mentioned that they had been baked by the up-and-coming renowned feminist sculptor Judy Chicago—pregnant with Beluga, that he was offered, and from thence tried to become a wall-flower in a room full of aggressive kudzu—professional women of every size and shape.

From somewhere across the room, above the general uproar, he heard his mother's voice, a dentist's drill hitting metal, saying, "It makes me furious to think what these old-boy networks get away with. Look at the Masters in Augusta! No women allowed, my ass! Why, that mighty woman athlete, the great Babe Didrickson Zaharias could've whipped every one of those fat-assed, pot-bellied, dong-brained, male chauvinist pigs at golf or anything else. She could kick ass! It simply infuriates me. No women! They'll rue the day!"

Along with the Champagne and cookies, Serge had somehow acquired a flyer stating the purpose of this gathering. ". . . to make the old-boy networks rue the day. . ." he read, glancingly, " . . . to pay tribute to the Great Tallulah Bankhead, our Lunar Mother of the Month, who went about naked in the Twenties, fearlessly, sweeping men underfoot like so much trash . . ."

Occasionally, the donkey-eyed head of a male feminist floated by as if on a pike, wearing an enthusiastic rictus for a smile. Like himself, these poor souls no doubt belonged to some powerhouse of a woman. Then someone started chanting "Women power! Women power!" Serge recognized the plangent voice of his Auntie Hoover, "She-Who-Must-Be-Obeyed," she who subjected Serge's attic room, or garret, as he preferred to think of it, to random searches for any indicators of masculine mischief, such as "Playboy" magazines, jockstraps, or condoms, she who had driven him from his secret meditations, from his poetry, and out into the cruel world—a basso profundo whose notability in any crowd could only be outdone by his mother's cry of "FURIOUS!" *Her* voice was even more irritating to him than Auntie Hoover's. He could feel his heart screaming in his chest every time he heard it.

His mother, Hettie Freed, and Bettina Battle gathered around the gleaming pink piano—an extraordinary instrument, Serge now noticed, because its three carved wooden legs were those of a woman in high heels.

Hettie Freed asked for the crowd's attention. She told them that Janet Hoover had a few words for them.

"Clear the way!" Bettina cried, making a path to the piano for Auntie Hoover. Bettina liked to be close to power—her motto was: "It's valuable to have a wise companion, and wiser to have a valuable one"—and Auntie Hoover was a valuable companion.

Bettina had thrown her arm over Auntie Hoover's shoulder and was reluctant to release her, but was forced to do so as Auntie Hoover, tank-like, ground her way up the piano stool and onto the piano to address the room from the mount, so to speak. She stood like a mighty

Maillol, arms akimbo, and waited for the crowd to recognize her position of authority. One member of the crowd did, immediately, and shouted, "O mighty woman, empower us all!"

"At each of our monthlies we gather to pay tribute to a mighty woman of the past. To-night we are going to honor the great actress and free spirit, the late and great Tallulah Bankhead. Hand me that poster," Auntie Hoover ordered, and a life-sized cardboard cut-out with a bracing flap was passed up to her from the crowd. She stood it next to her, stood at attention, and saluted it. It was a cutout of the naked Tallulah, done in the style of Augustus John, wearing only a string of pearls, along with other natural products of woman-kind.

"Some of you younger members of the Lunar Society might not know the great Tallulah, but for those of us who have battled long and hard for women's rights, this ballsy, outspoken dame, inventor of camp itself, has long been an inspiration."

"The naked truth," a female voice whis-pered in Serge's ear. He looked around but recognized no one in the crowd.

Serge leaned on a pedestal that held a bronze statuette of Atalanta determinedly pierc-ing a boar. He squinted at the little face of the boar and thought that it resembled himself in its

agony. Then his agoraphobic narcolepsy over-
came him.

He fell asleep until his ribs were poked.
How long he had slept he had no idea, but he
woke to the tune of "The Battle Hymn of the
Republic," only the words were those of the
"Women's Anthem."

Glory, Glory, Hail Tallulah!
Glory, Glory, Hail Tallulah!
Glory, Glory, Hail Tallulah!
Her Truth comes marching on.

"Hip, Hip, Hooray!" shouted the crowd,
which was uproarious now with inspiration and
Champagne.

Auntie Hoover addressed the gathering,
saying, "We must adopt Sheila Michaels's sug-
gestion that we refer to ourselves as 'Ms.' No
more prissy 'Miss' or downtrodden 'Mrs.'"
She beamed to the applause this inspired.

"How do you say that?" someone called.
"I see it here in the flyer. But it hasn't got a
vowel."

"Screw the vowel movement," roared
Auntie Hoover. "That's just a lot of masculine
crap. Just shout 'Mizzzzzzzzz' for all the world
to hear and take notice."

"What exactly would be the plural, do you
think?" the voice asked. "Mize?"

"Screw plural!" shouted Auntie Hoover. "Screw vowels! Just don't screw men." She whooped and the others joined in.

"I saw by the look on your face that 'The Women's Anthem' inspired you," purred the same soft voice that had whispered "the naked truth" in Serge's ear. "You looked so lonely, standing over here by yourself, I thought I'd bring you a fresh glass of Champagne. My name's Amanda Quaint. I know who you are. You're Serge Bering-Strait, the writer. I've read a couple of your pieces in *Women's Omnibus*."

She was a foot taller than he and wore a Mary Quant mini-skirt; but, somehow, she didn't frighten him. Most of the women he knew did. Amanda Quaint's voice was soft, forgiving.

He took the stemmed glass from her fingers—such pretty, well-manicured fingernails, such a nice shade of pink—and looked up at her; but he only had two hands and found himself awkwardly in possession of two glasses, the flyer, and his Plutarch, all of which he began to shuffle, or, more nearly, juggle.

Amanda Quaint said, "Here, let me take that. Why are you reading Plutarch? Are you taking a course?"

"Of course not." He blushed at his timid, almost inadvertent pun. "Everyone should know the lives of these extraordinary Greeks and Romans. Their parallel lives. The Anabasis and Katabasis—"

"Yes, I know all about that," she said. "I think that's Xenophon."

"You do?" His admiration for her lifted another notch. She took the empty glass and the flyer from him and managed to make them disappear while keeping her big violet eyes fixed on him. Her grace amazed him, her beauty gave him palpitations. "My name is Serge," he said.

"Yes, I know," she said.

"You're Amanda Quaint," he said.

"Yes, I know," she said.

"I'm sorry," he said.

"What have you got to be sorry for?"

He tightened his lips and shook his head. "I don't know. Sleeping on duty, maybe. I just feel sorry all the time."

"I didn't know you would be so shy," she said. "I read your beautiful poem on the F Train—'The Naked Truth?' Until this morning, I didn't know you were also a poet. A very romantic poet, at that! A little old-fashioned, but I like that. I like the old romantic poets much better than the Beats."

His eye-beams, through his horn-rims, rolled down to her open-toed pumps and back to her head, a crown of gold. He recalled

Yeats's lines, "That only God, my dear, could love you for your self alone and not your yellow hair?"

His attraction for her was instantaneous, chemical, genetic, he might have said, as if they had been brought together from the ends of the universe by Mother Nature herself, as if she had always been there in his very marrow, though his body was much too small for such a woman to have got into. In short, it was love at first sight.

"I think you're just brilliant!" Amanda Quaint said. "Men with brains and sensitivity turn me on." Serge didn't like the phrase, "turn me on," but it sounded sweet coming from Amanda Quaint. When Bettina had said much the same thing, during the drive downtown, it had sounded ravishing, a vulture's voluptuous hunger.

Embarrassed, he blurted out, "Benjamin Franklin said that a man's arm was just long enough to lift a glass of wine to his mouth," and drank off half the new glass of Champagne.

He was afraid to look in Amanda's eyes, for fear that they would not show responsiveness. "Quaint? Are you related to the Wiener King? I saw his balloon this morning."

"He's my grandfather," she said.

Serge looked up toward the ceiling as if in search of the giant red advertising phallus.

When he looked down, Amanda Quaint was gone.

Then he saw her being pulled off through the crowd by Bettina Battle. The angel of his desire was being kidnapped right out from under his wiener-focused nose.

Bettina had seized Amanda by the arm and dragged her off, kidnapped her from Serge, in order to offer Amanda double her current salary to join the staff of *Women's Omnibus*.

"We're looking for some new concepts," Bettina said, pulling Amanda away. "Sir Gay doesn't get it. He's a young fogey—never would have come up with an idea like your sky-mirrors."

"I think he's just brilliant," said Amanda, "and cute, too."

"Don't get any ideas. That Nancy boy is my poodle. But, if you accept my offer—*entre nous*, I'm leaving to go into politics and the company is looking for a new editor—you might end up being his boss. Then he can be your poodle. But, listen, it's too noisy to talk in here. Come on outside to my limo. We can talk there. Bring your drink. Now what I want, darling, is for you to give two weeks notice to your present employer and join us at *Women's Omnibus* in a fortnit."

Bettina Battle had Amanda Quaint all to herself in her limo now. A signal from Bettina had set the wheels in motion.

"Wait!" cried Amanda. "I wanted to say good-night to Serge."

"Roll on!" Bettina ordered her chauffeur, and seized Amanda by the knee. "How would you like to replace me as editor of *Women's Omnibus* when I go on to bigger and better things? Eh, Sweetie, answer me that!"

Amanda lifted Bettina's hand from her knee.

"Bloody Hell!" cried Bettina. "If you don't learn a little flexibility, you'll never get anywhere."

"I'll take my chances," said Amanda. "And keep your hands off me, if you don't want this glass of Champagne ruining your makeup."

"Listen, dear lady, I have a Black Belt in Karate."

"Watch out someone doesn't hang you by it."

Bettina Battle looked ruefully at Amanda and roared again to her driver: "ROLL ON!"

Back at the meeting of the Lunar Society, Serge felt bereft by his loss of Amanda Quaint.

He felt like going home to his garret at the top of his family's house and having a good cry over a nice, romantic, melancholy poem—

maybe something apropos by Poe—say, "Annabel Lee."

But then he tried to look on the sunny side, as an old song encouraged. At least he had escaped being escorted home by the insatiable, black-belted "Battle of Britain." But having escaped "the Battle of Britain" meant that Serge was abandoned to the tender mercies of his mother and Auntie Janet Hoover.

<u>2</u>

By eight o'clock, they were walking the misty streets of Greenwich Village. His mother pinched his left ear. She was furious at something that he had inadvertently said at the Lunar Society. The tired tongue of his tired mind had tied the title "Mister" Freed to "Miz" Freed in his good-bye. Pulling on his ear was a nasty habit of hers. His ears were always red and sore from her gripping digits. From boyhood, he saw cauliflower in his future. And Auntie Hoover held his right hand with a rock-crushing grip. They lifted him over a puddle.

His Auntie Hoover carried his scuffed Plutarch, at some point complaining about the state of the book's jacket and comparing it to the state of his London Fog, which, she reminded him, was her birthday gift to him.

She berated Serge for his carelessness, but he paid little attention, for he was used to being treated like a child by these two large and bullying women.

His mother nodded agreement with his Auntie Hoover in her assessment of him. It made her furious, she asserted, *furious*, that he was still such an incompetent child. Fortunately, most of this washed right off his rumpled London Fog. He had heard it all before, and, anyway, nothing could erase the image, seen through his misty glasses, of Amanda Quaint's seven-inches-above-the-knee, mini-skirted form from his hormone-drenched brain, his post-pubescent, testosterone-soaked soul. Fecklessly, he tugged for freedom, but they were too powerful.

Serge had grown up in the Village, had lived in the same five-story brownstone on Bethune Street all his life. The house had been passed down from his grandparents to his mother and four aunts. The family had made its money in brassieres. "Uplift by Updike." The slogan alone had made them a fortune in the Forties. Serge did not fail to see the irony in this, since his mother was famous for bra-burning.

Serge came to recognize a number of ironies and oddities about his family as he grew up. His Auntie Janet Updike had married a man named Hoover, who had run away from their honeymoon, so it was said, the only residue of this vanishing act being Auntie Janet's last name. The other three sisters, Charlotte, Emily, and Annie, were ink-stained spinsters who ran Boadicea Press out of the ground floor of the five-story brownstone. Serge heard it bruited about that they had once tried their hand at show business, as a trio, but were no match for Motown, and surrendered quietly to a non-vocal lifestyle. Occasionally, while they worked, they harmonized such tunes as "There's No Business Like Show Business," but when noticing that Serge was with them, fell into silence.

He would have described them as taciturn, if asked. Like many other failed artists, they had turned to politics. Their purpose was not money but a passion for causes, activism, anarchism, and general intellectual mayhem. They were as clever at stirring the pot as the three Shakespearean witches. Boadicea Press turned out what they referred to as "edification for the masses."

Even his friends, most of whom were

themselves from artistic, bohemian, or eccentrically rich backgrounds, teased him about the oddness of his family, and made common comment about the women being so big and him being so small, so undersized and frail, wondering to his face, often enough, as to whether he was adopted.

And then, by her maternalism toward him, some might have thought him to be the son of their Puerto Rican housekeeper and cook, had they not known that that was impossible. Because his young friends were almost sure that the crazy Hispanic drag queen who tended him with such devotion, could not have given birth. Or could he?

Even the family's living arrangements seemed odd to those visitors who ventured into the upper regions of the house. His mother and Auntie Hoover had rooms on the third floor, the three Boadicea aunties had rooms on the fourth, and Serge shared the fifth floor servants' quarters with Juanna Donna Lorca, the transgender who ambulated about the house in high heels and flamboyant female costumes and dominated their domestic life.

It was as if the sisters were trying to put the thought of a male, boy or young man, as far from their minds as possible, even if compelled to admit his existence. At times he felt like Mr. Rochester's closeted first wife in Jane Eyre.

But now, as he traversed the foggy rain-gleaming streets of Greenwich Village, his American Paris, on wobbly knobbly legs, he yearned for that hot little garret where he could at last be alone with his dreams of romantic love. Was Amanda Quaint to be La Belle Dame Sans Merci? Or was she as generous and open-hearted as he hoped, as her wide violet eyes would suggest?

As they approached the house, they saw that Juanna Donna Lorca and her twin brother Hector Alonzo de la Lorca were arguing on the sidewalk where a little group of neighbors and passers-by had gathered to watch, including his Boadicea aunties. The rubbernecking was un-derstandable, even forgivable, considering the show the Spanglish twins were putting on.

Juanna Donna screamed like an excited cockatoo and Hector growled like an angry bear. The front door of the house stood open, suggesting that Juanna Donna had pushed Hector out of it and down the front steps, sug-gesting it because Juanna Donna was still push-ing Hector away from the house, backing both of her straight arms with her considerable bulk. Everyone thought of Juanna Donna as "her," not "him."

Hector raised his fist and dropped it and raised it again and dropped it again, sorely tempted. "I no wanna hit you, so stop pushing me," he said. "How would it look, me hitting a woman, because that's what you look like?"

"But it don't bother you come here and ask a woman for money; it don't bother you that I been saving all my life to have my dong removed."

"You are a disgrace to all us Spanish males!" cried Hector, who, except for his mustache and masculine garb, looked just like Juanna Donna, with his square, handsome face and short husky body. But there was another difference between them. Juanna Donna had had a nose job, giving hers a ski-slope tilt, while Hector's nose was straight and a bit flat, like a handsome boxer.

"It reflects on me!" Hector shouted. He looked imploringly at the onlookers. "This thing is my brother. Would you believe it? My *twin* brother!"

"But I be your sister as soon as I have save enough money! No longer will I be Juanna Donna, half man, half woman. Then I will be Doña Juannadonna, a true lady. But you will never be Don Hector because you are no gentleman, no hidalgo, no true caballero!"

"You drag queen!" shouted Hector. "The shame! The disgrace!"

"The shame of a man who only come to his sister for money to pay gambling debts!"

The fortyish twins squared off and circled

each other like boxers. Hector's cuff links glittered, as did Juanna Donna's innumerable bracelets. The ruffled train of her black and purple Bata de Cola flamenco gown swept the sidewalk, becoming a damp rag. Her mantilla, caught on one large earring, flew like a cape, and her pumps clicked on the sidewalk as she circled Hector. "Punch my knobs and I break you neck!" cried Juanna Donna, who had been taking hormones for years.

Hector paused to straighten his powder-blue tie, dropping his hands to do so, and Juanna Donna released a straight right to his chin.

"Son-of-a-bitch," he cried. "I didn't think you'd hit me. Look, everybody, I want you to know this is a man I am fighting with—a drag queen maybe, but a man just the same—and I have every right to hit back." And he did—right on the tip of Juanna Donna's ski-slope, Bob Hope nose.

"Now you've just gone too far," shouted Auntie Hoover, stepping into the fray and walloping Hector left and right with Serge's Plutarch, a heavy if tattered tome.

While Juanna Donna and Hector were evenly matched, being twins, after all, Hector was no match for Auntie Hoover, who came at him like some kind of war machine, backing him up and finally causing him to turn and run from her onslaught, much to the amusement of the crowd, who hooted, cheered, and applauded. "Female assertiveness—" she said, looking after him, "macho men are no match for empowered women."

As if to emphasize what she said, the defective alarm of Schloch's Delicatessen down the street went off, sounding like a screeching banshee, and one could see from Hector's body language that it terrified him. He may have believed himself pursued by Auntie Hoover, a tank with a siren. He ducked into the sanctuary of the first bar in sight, Rocky's Rendezvous.

Juanna Donna felt some satisfaction in her knowledge that Hector had entered a gay bar. The last laugh was on him. Schloch's alarm stopped screaming with a final gurgle, and peace was reinstated on Bethune Street.

In the house, in the kitchen, holding a hanky to her bloody nose, Juanna Donna said, "I hopes you no expect no food from me. I'm nobody's Sancho Panza. You Quixotes get yourselves some queki de limón, if you wants."

After checking Juanna Donna's nose and seeing that there was no real harm done, Serge's mother and four aunties busied themselves at the unfamiliar domestic task of making tea and serving themselves cake. They sat at the long kitchen table, like a group of irritated firemen just in from a chemical burnout.

"Put your head down between your legs," Dagmar advised Juanna Donna. "Isn't that a good cure for a nose bleed?" she asked Auntie Hoover.

Auntie Hoover said, "Boxers put their heads back." Auntie Hoover was a boxing aficionado. The three Boadicea Aunties devoured their lemon cake, making masticating sounds of supreme satisfaction.

No help from that direction.

Juanna Donna's eyes flashed at them. She pulled a bloody paper towel away from her nose and said, "Ain't any of you got normal female nursing instincts like Juanna Donna, whose brain has been marinated in estrogen? O.K." she added, "you're all testosterone titties, but then you could at least be gentlemen. A gentleman would help me. ¿Ya no hay nobles hidalgos ni bravos caballeros, who can protect us females? They have all left it to you Auntie Hoover to act like a real he-man, out on the street at least. But not in here!"

She watched in disgust as Auntie Hoover heeded nothing but cake. "You'll see," she cried, "I won't cook nothing 'round here for a week, and you all starve and see if I care. Some gentlemen, some true caballeros! Bad pipples, I say." She looked at Serge with disgust in her burning eyes.

"Bad pipples! I got to take care of my nose," she told him, as she staunched the flow of blood with a new handful of paper towels. "Oh, my God!" she shouted, "there is blood on my beautiful mantilla. I have wipe my nose with it. I have to soak it, queek." She headed for the upper regions of the house.

"I have an idea for a story about a brave caballero," Serge told her, following in her wake, "a real *macho* man. I've been thinking about it for some time and I'm going to call him Resurgius."

"What kind of name is that?" she asked, turning to him on the staircase.

"Dog Latin for a resurgent Serge, a comeback kid."

"Comeback from where?" she asked, still holding a wad of paper towels to her nose.

"From being pecked raw, Juanna Donna, that's where. Can I have a few of those peppy-steppy pills you're always popping when you clean? I'm going straight to my room and get started, and I need some pep. I've had a long, exhausting day, but, boring as it sometimes was, aggravating as it sometimes was, it was also inspiring, because . . . I fell in love today—love at first sight—and so, at last, I've got the heroine of my book to further my inspiration—someone to put on a pedestal and look up to; and I need my energy tonight; while it's all hot in my brain. Energy! I'm determined to get started right away. Right now! Tonight!"

Juanna Donna reached in her skirt pocket and filled Serge's palm with little red pills. "You can hop all night on these little red diablos," she said. "Once I stay up for a week. Remember that time when I clean the whole house and everybody get mad at me because I threw everything out? It was them diablos."

"But I'm afraid, Juanna Donna. I'm afraid I won't have the will or the energy to come home every night and work on this book. Writing a novel is a marathon. I'm just not sure I can maintain the discipline required. That's why I want you to do something special for me. I want you to promise me that you won't let me weaken, that you'll make me write every night, until I'm done, that no matter how tired I say I am, or how tired you think I am, you will help me to complete my task. Swear it!"

"Suppose I has to box your ears or throw bucket of cold water in your face?"

"No matter what you have to do, just don't let me weaken."

"These I swear to, cross my heart and hopes to die. See, nothing crossed 'cept my toes stuffed in these pumps, but I can't help that. I will be your second will, I swear before God and Puerto Rico. Now, get busy! Hit those keys!"

Serge took the pills and went into his room. Soon the little red diablos made him feel as if he had a rocket in his brain. He was lifting off.

He stripped to his polka-dot boxer shorts and sat down at his desk.

Outside his open window, before which sat his broken air-conditioner, there was a God-like roll of thunder, and rain swished down from above in silver streaks like swords.

A breeze wafted in and his brain was alive, inspired. He wanted to bang out the title of his proposed opus in caps so large that the world could not fail to read them. But, disappointed at the size of the typed caps of his title, he took up a marking pencil and furiously printed across the top of the page and underlined—

<u>RESURGIUS</u>

<u>3</u>

"You look kinda droopy," said Bettina Battle. "I hope you've been burning the midnight oil on that UNIVAC article. How's it coming?"

"Oh, coming right along," said Serge, looking at her through bleary eyes and blurry glasses. She was barring the entrance to his cubicle and he imagined how a caged guinea pig must feel. She didn't even provide him with a nowhere wheel to run on. Bettina loomed over him like Wonder Woman about to lasso an evil-doer. Her incredulity was tangible. She waited, threateningly, with the patience of a cat playing with a mouse, and Serge said, "Really, Bettina, it's going fine."

"It had better be," she warned, turning to scan the enormous room full of workers like a sniper seeking a target, beading in on one here and one there with telescopic and predatory phthalo-green eyes. Serge knew that further reference would be made. She turned back to Serge. "Have you given any more thought to my offer?"

"I thought about it most of the night. It kept me awake. I only had two hours sleep, so, if I look droopy, it's your fault."

"Come back to my office later if you need some Scotch in your coffee." As if in the throes of a drug-induced hallucination, Serge saw the mask of her face morph from iron warning to lascivious rubber invitation. He blinked in an effort to focus, then saw her toss him a wink as she went on to her next harassment, the object of which might be male, female, or potted plant.

He wanted to do as Juanna Donna had ordered and call Amanda Quaint, but he was very much afraid that she would reject him. Bettina Battle, attractive as she was, simply turned him off. Her subdermal coldness and raptor-like aggressiveness made her seem anything but a beautiful woman. Rather more a bird of prey.

He wasn't often pursued by beautiful

women. He wasn't often pursued by women at all—except for his mother and aunties, whose pursuit of him was like that of a riot squad. He remembered a love-struck stick-figure of a girl in grade school, and didn't a young woman once wink at him on the subway? Or had she caught a bit of dust in her eye? He had always preferred to think that she had winked. But it was a strange fix he found himself in, being pursued by a beauty who gave him the sinking sense of a green-eyed monster.

Now on the other hand, Amanda Quaint was easily as beautiful as Bettina Battle but radiated a tolerant kindness, "a glad kindness," as Yeats had put it in a poem, that, strangely enough, made him even more afraid of her than of Bettina Battle. Just what was this fear he felt? Well, he knew, didn't he? It was the fear of rejection. Why should such a lovely and decent young woman want a little skinny sack of bones like him? Bettina Battle would devour whatever was put before her, but Amanda Quaint was a woman of taste and discrimination—she liked his poetry—and so would fastidiously pick and choose.

He trembled at the thought of making the phone call that Juanna Donna had ordered him to make on pain of a spanking. How could he muster the courage? He must play the man, the he-man, the hero. He must be Resurgius! Fearlessly, Resurgius would pick up the phone and call.

Serge dialed for an outside line. He dialed the number of Amanda Quaint's office. When a voice came on the line, he said in his own cracked voice, "Amanda Quaint, please."

"Whom shall I say is calling?" said a quick New York accent.

"*Re-sur-gi-us*," he said, his voice cracking like a fourteen-year-old's. "No, no, no—I'm sorry, I got confused—tell her it's Serge Bering-Strait." And by this act of derring-do was actual magic in the form of electrical sparks produced on the line and the voice of Amanda Quaint poured like honey into his right ear, "Hello, Serge! I've been hoping you'd call me."

Oh, the wizardry of Edison! Faraday and Electricity! It was the voice of his beloved!

> *Mary had a little lamb*
> *Whose fleece was white as snow*
> *And everywhere that Mary went*
> *The lamb was sure to go!*

Was it the telephone or the Victrola? It was Edison, wasn't it? Serge was rattled.

"Is that you, Serge? Where are you?"

"_____"

Serge, for a hair-raising instant, could not

speak. Then, his wild reddish hair settling on his head as after a bout with one of Tesla's electric arcs, he squeaked—

"Yes, yes, I'm here." And now so were the words—"I was wondering would you—could you—do you think we might—what I mean is—"

"I'd be delighted to meet you after work. Would you come over to Rockefeller Plaza and meet me? I'll be behind the statue of Prometheus. Shall we say sixish?"

"Abso . . . abso . . ."

"Absolutely," said Amanda Quaint. "I'll be waiting."

And true to her trueness, just as Serge Bering-Strait had known her nature to be honorable and trustworthy, there she was waiting behind the glistening, fountain-wet buns of the golden statue of Prometheus. Yes, Prometheus had brought fire and there she was, the flame in his heart, looking even more beautiful than he could remember, her blonde hair in a golden French twist, a white lace blouse tenting her ample bosom, her Mary Quant mini valancing unimpeachable legs, her pink-peeping open-toed pumps heeled five up, and, most striking of all, her violet eyes seeking him in the crowd that seemed to be sucking up all the air around him. How was he to speak to her without air with which to waft his words?

"Serge! I'm so happy to see you! Why do you look at me like that?" she asked, looking down at him. "Are you hungry?"

Hungry for the lips of my desire, Serge might have answered with Ernest Dowson's words but didn't.

"I'm famished," said Amanda, taking his arm and leading him hastily around to the front of the al fresco restaurant and down its steps. They were seated at a table from which vantage they could see Manship's bronze, gold-leafed statue of Prometheus stealing fire from the gods as a gift for humankind in all its full frontal glory. To Serge, it was the very vision of Resurgius, his hero. Behind Prometheus, the seventy-story RCA Building towered up and into cloud-piercing invisibility, the late sun peeling the skyscraper's façade, huge shadows wavering up its vanishing height.

The polyphonic chatter of countless voices, accompanied by the flappings of the flags of all nations, did not make their own words indistinct, for Serge and Amanda were focused on each other. Serge said excitedly, "I started a novel. Well, maybe it's just a no-vella—maybe it's going to be kind of short, I'm not sure. I guess it all depends on what happens next. It's going very fast," he rushed on, "now that I'm on to it."

"What's it called? What's it about?"

"The hero is named Resurgius, and he looks like that Prometheus, all golden muscles, not like me at all, and it isn't autobiographical like so many first novels. No, it's a work of the imagination. It's futuristic. But it's a love story, for sure. Resurgius is the kind of guy who never has to say he's sorry."

"But he'll say it if he should, won't he?"

"Sure, he's not afraid."

"Can I read it when you're done?"

"You'll be the first, Amanda, because I trust your judgment."

"Really? It's so sweet of you to say so."

The waiter brought them their drinks—a Whiskey Sour for Serge and a Screwdriver for Amanda.

"Cheers!" said Amanda. Then she put her drink down. "How exciting that you've begun a novel. I'm facile enough for articles, but I could never dream of writing a novel. But you—you being a poet—I bet the words just cascade from you."

"Well, sometimes they just dribble. But don't underrate yourself," said Serge. "Your article on sky-mirrors is one of the things that inspired my novel."

"Really? How thrilling! But you know, I was assigned to write that article and, in truth, thought the whole idea was crazy. I, for one, like to sleep at night. It's plain nutty! Just another way of getting more work out of us poor peons."

"Gee," said Serge, "I thought there was something romantic about it."

"And that's what I mean about you," Amanda picked up enthusiastically, "like all real poets you see romance in everything. You have a romantic heart. That's what I love about your poetry—

> The night's an Arab's sheet
> Of swirling blue and black.
> The earth is at his feet,
> The stars are at his back.

Oh, it gives me goosebumps! Did anybody ever tell you that you look like a skinny Dylan Thomas? All that wild red hair, and that cute little bulbous nose. If only it were red, too, then you'd look just like him, but I don't suppose you drink enough."

"I had three Whiskey Sours in a row one night!"

"*Did* you? Well, I really wouldn't want to be friends with a boy who drank too much, even if he was a poet."

"I'm only going to have one—now."

"After we eat, shall we take a walk?"

"Where to?"

"Oh—uptown—maybe up to Central Park. It's such a beautiful early autumn evening. I love autumn, don't you?"

"Oh yes," Serge said. He would have loved anything that she loved. For he loved her more each instant that they were together.

"Tell me about yourself," Amanda said later, as they joined the flow up Fifth Avenue, toward Tiffany's and on up to the Plaza Hotel and Central Park. He had to reach up to hold her arm, his thin fingers gripping a solid bicep. The power of her beautiful body thrilled him.

"I'm twenty-three years old," he said, "and a graduate of NYU School of Journalism."

"What's your family like?"

"Women."

"What?"

"All women. I have a mother and four aunties."

"Oh, yes, I know who your mother is, and I know your Auntie Janet Hoover. They're famous in lib circles. You say you have three other aunts?"

"Yes. Charlotte, Emily, and Annie. They run Boadicea Press."

"Oh, we all know Boadicea Press. I read a number of their books when I was taking Women's Studies at Harvard. Let me see . . . there was *The Tyrannical Male, Football Wives,* and *Beaten Down and Beaten Up.*

Those are a few of the titles I remember. Personally, I think they're a little extreme. I have a grandfather, a father, and three brothers who are almost as sweet as you are. I don't think we have to defame the whole male sex just because of the misbehavior of a few."

"That's my point," said Serge enthusiastically. He was almost swinging by her arm and tap-dancing as he tried to turn and look up at her. She took such long strides. Strident, that was her walk, strident—but she was so sweet.

"That's my point exactly," Serge repeated, "that you don't defame a whole sex just because you've got a mad on at a few members of it. Men say derogatory things about women, too, but they're doing the same thing. They're stereotyping. They're not trying to understand. I try to be fair-minded."

"As do I."

"I can tell. A lot of women don't, though, don't try. A lot of women just think men are no good, especially nowadays, with the Women's Movement in full swing. Wow, I grew up seeing the whole thing from the female point of view. The only masculine point of view I got at home was from Juanna Donna, who is more of a woman than a man, at least nowadays. On the other hand, I really hardly knew my mother—hardly *know* her. My real mother, the mother who raised me—well, I know it sounds crazy—has been a transexual man who was much more maternal than my birth mother.”

“My goodness! Tell me about it.”

“Well, Juanna Donna’s our housekeeper. She even taught me Spanish, or, what you might call, Spanglish, a mixture of Spanish and English. Juanna Donna came from Puerto Rico just about the time I was born and got a job as our housekeeper and really became my nanny, although in those days he called himself Juan de la Lorca, or so I’ve been told. He calls himself Juanna Donna, nowadays, and, to tell you the truth, I’ve always called him—or her—that, and I’m not a bit sure what his real name is, really. I’m pretty sure her last name is Lorca, though, like the poet.”

“Garcia Lorca?”

“Right. But she’ll always be Juanna Donna to me. I think I named her that when I was a kid and everybody started calling her that. But Juanna Donna’s no poet.” He put a hand on his heart. “Poet or not, male or female, she’s like a mother to me. Sometimes I think the male can have more maternal instincts than the female, at least that’s been my experience— and bigger boobs!”

“There’s truth in what you say,” said Amanda. “I bet you’d make a wonderful father. Even now, I’m writing an article on the more extreme forms of feminism, which I call—the article, I mean—'Have Some Feminists Gone Too Far?' It poses the question whether a small group of libbers—and remember, I consider myself a serious libber—want social equality—equal pay, for instance, for equal work, or actually want superiority; whether we want—or should I say *they* want—loving relationships with men or no men at all. At times it seems as if the latter is the truth of the matter.

"Take the case of Valerie Solanas, the founder and only member of S.C.U.M., the Society for Cutting Up Men. I've read something she wrote and it's absolutely insane. She sent me a manuscript, hoping, I guess, that I had some pull and could get it published in one of the magazines. I was free-lancing at the time. Poor thing! She's bound to wind up doing herself or someone else some harm. We libbers are not all like her! I don't like the idea of some women speaking for other women. We're independent thinkers, each and every one of us, or should be."

"How wonderful!" cried Serge, bouncing along beside her, enthralled by her words, only vaguely aware that they were approaching Fifty-Ninth Street and Central Park South, walking just to be walking and talking—"Because my novel is a spoof on the very extremists of whom you speak. I try to keep it amusing, but thinking of them can still hurt a fellow."

"That's because you're a poet and are so highly sensitive," said Amanda, "but you mustn't let yourself become bitter. There's so much sweetness in life and you must try to focus on that."

"Oh, it's O.K.. I haven't the strength for much bitterness."

"But you must keep your spirit up. You must not slump."

"I stand erect when I'm with you."

"That's quite a compliment. Look," Amanda cried, "we've walked all the way up to the Hotel Plaza. Look," she cried again, excitedly, "the Hansom cabs are waiting across the way. Shall we go for a ride through the Park?"

"Amanda, my dear, they are not Hansom cabs, no matter what they tell the tourists. A Hansom cab has two wheels, seats two people, and the driver rides in back. You must have seen them in a Sherlock Holmes movie. These are four wheeled carriages and the driver drives from the front. See that fellow?"

"Yes, I can see what you mean." She laughed, "You certainly have a didactic streak in you."

"I'm sorry," he said, "I'm always trying to get things straight in my own mind. But that fellow!" He pointed to the first carriage driver in a queue of carriages. "That carriage driver is Juanna Donna's brother, Hector."

"How interesting," said Amanda.

"That's Juanna Donna's *twin* brother."

"That's her twin? He doesn't look a bit feminine to me."

"Juanna Donna had her nose done and has been taking hormones for years. She has boobies and wears dresses, the fancier the better. I guess you could say she's left her twinship. This was probably how she looked when I first knew her but I can't remember that far back."

"He looks very macho . . . except for the love beads."

"Yes," said Serge, "that's something different."

They had approached within a few steps of Hector's carriage and Hector had recognized Serge and called out, "Sergey, qué passe? Are you come up here to take the beautiful lady for a ride through the park?"

Hector jumped down from the carriage. He was wearing a top hat and carried a buggy whip. "Please meet my wonderful old horsy, Hidalgo, a true gentleman." Hearing his name, Hidalgo turned his grey head toward them, fixed his big brown eyes on them, and whinnied. He looked old and tired and patient.

"What a sweet animal," said Amanda.

"Allow me to introduce myself, Señorita—Hector de la Lorca, at your service," at which he bowed to Amanda.

"This is Señorita Amanda Quaint," said Serge.

"Enchanté," said Hector, bowing again. He said, "It's best in French."

"Enchanté," Amanda responded.

"You are taking the señorita for a carriage ride through the park, are you not?"

"Oh, let's do," said Amanda. "It's so romantic."

The lights in the buildings all around them were coming on, one at a time and then in clusters. It was almost musical, the way they would run vertically or horizontally or then in a whole block of fifty or more windows, like the tentative beginnings and then the first full riffs of a symphony. Da-Da, Da, Da, Da, Da! And the tiny twinkles of the night lights in the darkening park could be seen across the way like lightning bugs.

"Will there be a moon out tonight?" Amanda asked Hector.

"When you get in the park the moon will be clear as a golden bell in the sky." He took her arm and helped her into the carriage. "If the señorita would not mind waiting for a moment while I speak to young Serge." And he turned to Serge, took his arm, and led him a few feet off from the carriage.

"Serge, my young friend, true son of my sister Juanna Donna Lorca, it has occurred to me that you might take pity on someone who is, after all, almost a member of your family, by blood, which is thicker than water, that you might consider helping me in my time of great distress.”

“Well,” said Serge, surprised by such a turn, “what can I do for you, Hector?”

“I have a gambling debt, so I borrow money from some people down on the docks who say my carriage and Hidalgo will be collateral for the loan. But the interest on the loan goes up so fast that the carriage and Hidalgo will not cover it. I ask them then what would happen if this should come to pass, and they say that I have knees, don’t I? By which I think they mean I will be harmed. If I could get them the money before the interest goes too far, this would save me bodily injury. Enough money would save my poor old Hidalgo and the carriage. As you know, I went to see Juanna Donna to ask her for help, but you saw what happened. She hit me.”

“But, Hector,” said Serge, “she is saving all her money for the big operation. You know what I mean. You know how important that is to her.”

“To become a woman,” said Hector sadly. “I know. But I am thinking when I see you, maybe out of your deep and abiding love for who is really like you mother you will help you uncle to set himself free of this terrible trap he is in."

"How big is this trap?"

"Fifteen Hundred Yankee Dollars would free Hector from a terrible fate."

"Fifteen Hundred Dollars! That's a lot of money, Hector."

"But you make good money, no? Is not so much for you, eh?"

"They really mean to hurt you?"

"They really mean to hurt me!"

"I have some savings," said Serge. He took out his checkbook and wrote Hector a check for what he needed to get himself out of trouble. He handed it to Hector. "You must promise me, Hector—no more gambling!"

"No more gambling, Señor! But you must promise me, please, please do not tell our Juanna Donna that you have lent me this money. She would be very angry. Now," said Hector, his voice lightening with relief, "I shall take you for the best, most romantic moonlight ride through Central Park that anyone has ever taken, with my compliments and Hidalgo's, at which Hidalgo turned his old gray head toward them and said something indecipherable and, no doubt, in equine Spang-lish.

Hector kept Amanda and Serge in the park for hours (over two hundred dollar's worth of ride, gratis), a great, stretch-marked moon overhead, pointing out places of interest like the Wollman Rink, the Sheep Meadow, the Pond, the Zoo, and the Carousel, and considerately falling silent and almost invisible when they came to dark stretches under cover of the leafy trees, the short dark tunnels, and the glowing high-arched bridges where he expected they needed privacy for petting and for the suction-cup snap-release of kisses, which he could hear between the clops of Hidalgo's echoing hooves.

They emerged from the park after midnight, drawing up before the splendiferous doors of the Plaza Hotel. Parting is such sweet sorrow, the Bard had told them both, and so, with one last kiss and reaching arms they said farewell. Amanda hailed a cab. Serge found a subway. Each dreamed of the other on the way home. At the stable on Tenth Avenue, Hector gave Hidalgo a cube of sugar and kissed him goodnight.

At home, Juanna Donna had waited up for Serge.

"What is the idea of coming in so late? How you gonna write tonight?"

"Oh, but I really want to write tonight! I have so much to say. My heart is full! Give me some of those little red diablos and dame una café, por favor—con leche! I'll write all night and believe me, Juanna Donna, I'll work all day tomorrow and feel like a new man, sans sleep, sans everything! I am inspired because I'm in love!" After changing into pajamas, bathrobe, and slippers, he sat down at his Olympia and began to conduct his symphony.

Coming up the stairs with a tray of coffee and a demitasse of little red diablos, Juanna Donna could hear the typewriter in action, like a syncopated clock.

<u>4</u>

39 Whitehall Street. So long as the Viet Nam war raged on, that infamous address struck terror into the heart of every young pacifist who was registered for the draft in the New York City area, and Serge Bering-Strait was no exception. A vaccine could prevent polio, but there was no way of being vaccinated against the draft, an epidemic that led to the crippling horrors of boot camp and perhaps even to death. And now Serge had been struck down in the very blossom of life. He dropped the brown

government envelope and wobbled down the hall from his room to Juanna Donna's room on afflicted legs. Thought was beyond him. Emotions, like a thousand stampeding cows, crushed reason under hoof. Instinct alone sent him to Juanna Donna, a terrified child to his mother, to his Madre/Padre, to be taken to her ample, estrogenized bosom and held in hirsute safety.

"There, there," said Juanna Donna, "you must no be afraid, leetle Serge," and she rocked his tearful being in her arms. "I see that nasty envelope when I take in the mail this morning and I know right away what it was. Maybe I should have call you at work. But I think maybe he want to be macho about this, maybe he want to act like that superhero he's writing about . . . what you call him?"

"Resurgius," he sobbed.

"Si, Resurgius! But I know a writer is different from a hero"—she patted his hair, pushed it back out of his eyes—"and Juanna Donna Lorca, she cry too. She cry all morning, but then she gets idea how to get you out of this if you want to get out of it."

Serge stepped back and looked at Juanna Donna, his tearful blue eyes flashing with hope. "How? Quick, how? Tell me before my knees buckle!"

"I know you are my proud leetle nooky man, but you must pretend you like other boys. You must pretend, my leetle macho niño, to be almost as gay as Juanna Donna," and she flourished her fan, cling-clanging her bracelets. "I know lots of gays who want to get in and they pretend to be straight, so you don't want to get in, you pretend to be gay. Simple, eh? You know me all your life. If I had started my hormones when you were leetle, I would have suckled you. Just act like me and say what I would say. I show you how."

The brown induction envelope with the voice of authority emanating from it ordered that Serge bring toothbrush and toilet articles to the Armed Forces Induction Center at 39 Whitehall Street on a Friday at 5:30 A.M. Early September had been unusually warm, summery, but now autumn had set in and a cool breeze flowed into the car from the open window on the passenger side. Juanna Donna drove, chattering away to keep Serge's mind off where they were going.

Bettina Battle had been informed that he might not appear at work that day—or, for that matter, a long time into the future. Serge had called Amanda Quaint as well. She had assented to write to him as soon as he could send his address—just in case anything went wrong. No "Dear Serge" letters, she promised. His mother and aunties had decided on protest and had left the house at three A.M. bound for Peter Minuit Plaza where a number of celebrities were expected to gather, placards and megaphones in hand. Old Beats, young Hippies, and Flower Children were out in full pacifistic force, carrying "Make Love, Not War" signs and chanting "Hell no, we won't go!"

Juanna Donna, wearing a long, multi-colored serape, jangling earrings, and made-up to look like a Ma Jode who had struck it rich, came prepared to join the protest. She found a place to park, some distance from the Induction Center, and they walked the rest of the way, soon finding themselves in the midst of protesters and mounted policemen. Among the protesters, in the twilight morning, Serge saw Doctor Spock of baby book fame, several actors whose names he couldn't place, and the bearded Beatnik poet Allen Ginsburg, who wore an orange batik shawl, a huge flowered tie, a rosary, and a Buddhist amulet. There were cymbals on his fingers, of the sort affected by Egyptian belly-dancers.

"I'm gonna get me some of those," said Juanna Donna, pointing at Ginsburg. "Now you remember what I tell you," she said, letting go of his hand like a mother sending her child off to kindergarten on the first day. He waved to his own mother and aunties, but they were too involved in their chant of "Hell no, Serge won't go!" to notice him as he entered the faded nine-story red brick building of 1886 construction with barricades like vampire's teeth at its mouthing Moloch-like entrance.

He was no longer Serge Bering-Strait, but one of many, as he stepped through an elevator door that bore the slogan "The Security of World Peace Starts Here." Soon he was stripped for his physical, during which brutal military medicos subjected him to a number of dehumanizing indignities, such as having him bend over while they stuck their rubberized fingers up his ass and felt around. It was horrible, but why hadn't he had those medical fingers up his ass when he needed them to make the required weight, which he failed to make by about a finger's worth—they had him stuff down a bananna and that qualified him—and yet it put him in the mood for Room 604, the psychiatrist's office.

Now he did as Juanna Donna had told him to do. He tried to behave like Juanna Donna, queen of high camp. He rolled a thin, feminine shoulder at the shrink, flirtatiously, and said, in an unnaturally high-pitched voice, "Hi, Big Boy," the very words Juanna Donna had told him to use. It wasn't easy, and it turned him red in the face, but still he said it, mortified, desperation being his king—or his QUEEN—at this most embarrassing moment. It was a question of do or die, so he did.

But what most injured his pride was that the shrink showed no doubt. "Gay," he said, with complete indifference. "Take this paper and go," and he stamped something on the paper. Serge felt as if the shrink had stamped "Gay" on his forehead.

When he left 39 Whitehall Street, a free woman—he meant MAN—relieved, happy, and ashamed, he saw his family being hauled off in a police van. Oh, well, it wasn't the first time that they had been hauled off in a Black Maria. But he had no one to tell that he had escaped the clutches of the military, death in Viet Nam, the end of Resurgius, the end of Amanda Quaint. Juanna Donna had been taken away as well and he had no way to get home because he could not drive, and, if he could, had no keys to the car anyway and so he must walk through the streets of lower Manhattan, the fingernail tip of the island, where no bar was open yet, and find a subway station. But where to go? It was still too early to go to work at *Women's Omnibus* in the American Rubber Climax Building—he shivered at the thought of rubber fingers adroitly invading his sanctum sanctorum and squeezed his pained self shut at the bottom—up tight though he may seem— and there was no one at home, his family by now, no doubt, behind bars, almost certainly singing, "We shall overcome."

The day grew light as he wandered, and, as he wandered, he wondered if he had done the right thing. He was distracted from his ruminations when he looked up at the early morning sky and saw the huge, familiar, still lighted wiener hovering overhead. The lights blinked on and off, reciting the mantra QUAINT-WIENERS-*QUAINT!*-O, Amanda! in many colors and in a fabulous syncopation. He only wished for Amanda's sake that he could be more like his hero, Resurgius, but, as Juanna Donna had said, a hero is one thing and a writer is another, seldom the same.

In Battery Park, he sat down on a dewy bench to give himself some horizon therapy, but the Statue of Liberty loomed before him and, like all women, fixed his attention. Now she was a proper mate for Resurgius, he thought, big, beautiful, and stalwart, leading the way with her torch, book in hand. Yo, Mama!

He could see Resurgius following her in adoration, just as he would follow Amanda Quaint. This was Friday and, on Monday, Amanda might start work at *Women's Omnibus*. He would see her all day every day from then on. O joy! And O joy, too, because he was free of the government! It did irritate him that the minions of government so readily believed him when he told them that he was gay. Then he wondered if they knew what they were doing—if they saw in him something that he didn't know was there. He was an aesthetic type of person, even a bit prim perhaps, yes, rather pale and prim and thin and proper; but no, he was mad for Amanda Quaint, so he couldn't be gay. What it was, was that Juanna Donna had so well instructed him as to how to act, and Juanna Donna was an expert on both sexes. Well, enough of that! It was the government that was crazy, calling him gay, not Juanna Donna.

*

The phone rang and rang. Standing in his cubicle, holding the receiver, Serge realized there was no one at home yet. Probably all still at the police station. He was anxious to let them know that he had escaped the military, especially Juanna Donna, who would be a happy little mother to hear it—a mamacita.

"New concepts!" cried Bettina Battle, her lower lip waving a spittle-stuck Virginia Slim cigarette like a baton. Serge could see and hear her vividly from across the enormous office which faded around her. He was no more than seated at his Selectric when she was upon him.

"Where's my UNIVAC III piece? I could have written the damn thing myself by now.

68

HOW UNIVAC WILL CHANGE WOMEN'S LIVES. Statistics Prove Women Superior to Men Any Old Day of the Week. Roll out the stats! What's the matter with you, Bering-Strait? You little twerp, you great twit! By the way, you're late! What's the meaning of dragging your skinny bum in here at Nine-fifteen?"

"I was almost drafted," he said. "Don't you remember? I told you I had to report for induction this morning."

"Well, when are they taking you?"

"They don't want me," he said, actual tears welling up in his eyes.

"Why not? Is there more than appears the matter with you?"

"I have a physical problem."

"What? Can't get it up? No balls? No dick? You certainly keep it zippered up!" She shouted so that the whole office could hear.

"Flat feet," he said, mortified.

"Flat head, more likely. New concepts come out of heads shaped like rockets," she shouted. "New concepts are ejaculations from erected heads. New concepts come like cum! Let me hear those fingers make music on that Selectric. I want to hear Mozart's Third Divertimento for the UNIVAC emanating from within your cubicle in five minutes."

She tugged the stuck Virginia Slim from her lower lip, waving a little spot of blood that dribbled down her chin vampirishly. "Hit those keys!" she cried, spraying tiny blood spots on his shirt. In a second he could hear her some distance away using the lash of her tongue on somebody else. He could hear the poor victim screaming inside his or her head, another lashed oarsman on the great pulsing trireme called *Women's Omnibus*.

Before he could write "Statistics show–" he was summoned to Bettina Battle's corner office. She leaned back in her pink padded swivel chair, another Virginia Slim stuck to her lip, her long legs and spiked heels up on her desk, and gave him a girlish smile as he entered. He closed the glass door behind him.

"Got anything on that . . . what is it you're working on?"

"UNIVAC. Statistics. Women are superior . . ."

"Got anything on that yet?" Her voice was soft and oleaginous.

"You just left me two minutes ago. I've hardly had time to get the paper in the machine."

"Sit down, Bering-Strait—Gay! Was I a bit harsh on you? I mustn't let anyone in the office see that I have favorites. You can understand that, can't you? You're not still crying, are you?"

"That wasn't about you. Just nerves from

the Induction Center."

"Oh, that's right. You were drafted or something—or was it that you were not drafted? Wait a minute. Let me sort it out. I know—you were not drafted because you have flat feet, right? But there's nothing else wrong with you, is there?"

"No, I'm fine."

"A little slow, maybe, eh?"

"I have an I.Q. of 168."

"But that's in male terms. That would only be about 68 in a woman. Still, you're a cute little fellow, and I've decided to take you to a play tonight. What do you think of that, hah?"

"I'm awfully tired already. I had to get up at three o'clock this morning to go in for induction."

"Say, isn't there some way we can use that as an advertising concept? Write something up and show it to me. MEN DRAFTED BY REASON OF INFERIOR INTELLECT. Something on that order. Now, about this play—it's called 'Oh! Calcutta!' and the actors take off their clothes in it. Wobbling breasts and dangling dongs all over the stage. Definitely a new concept. Eliminate the story and give us the naked truth. That's all people want anyway. They really want to go about sniffing at each other's rear ends like dogs, so let's get to it. This should put an end to all that old fashioned talkie trash that Tennessee Williams and old Eugene O'Neill wrote—and Shakespeare, my own countryman, he's the worst. Don't you agree?"

"I like Shakespeare," said Serge tentatively.

"Yes—but naked! To be naked, or not to be naked. That is the question. Sometimes costumes help, I admit, though. As your poem puts it, 'The naked truth will lie. The night's an Arab's sheet,' and all that shit. But a good looking bum is always a turn-on. What's a sycophant, Serge?"

"An ass-kisser."

"Even better, a brown-noser. That's what I mean about new concepts, Serge. New concepts! The world will never get anywhere without new concepts. I'll pick you up in my limo outside the building at closing time. Do you agree? I warn you, put a sock in your cake hole." She slammed a hand on her desk.

"Well that's settled. But remember, if you stand me up, I'm going to be very hurt. It's likely to bring out the bloody wrath in me." She winked, but Serge knew she meant business, and he couldn't afford to be fired just when Amanda Quaint was coming to work there.

"Of course I'm only ragging you, Serge. You know that, don't you, my little poodle? What, do I see more tears? Stop thinking about that nasty old Induction Center, will you? You're a free man now, no more Royal Marines. I've slept with all of them. Not a real man in the lot. O.K., buzz off and get me those stats! Oh, and that other thing—what was it?"

"An advertising concept from the Induction Center."

"Right! Find a product—food-on-a-stick for instance—and have all those naked inductees eating it while the doctors stick their rubberized fingers up their bum holes. You see that—I can come up with a new concept just like that," and she snapped her fingers, then pointed at the door. "Out, out, brief candle," she commanded, "I'm feeling conceptual."

While he worked, Serge constantly reminded himself that Disraeli had said that there were three kinds of lies; white, black, and statistical. He tried to shape UNIVAC's results to suit Bettina Battle's concepts, nodding off occasionally into that far land of Resurgius where he was king. Once he ripped a cigarette from Bettina Battle's lower lip and she bled to death, but something happened and he ended up saving her by pressing his shirt tail to her lip like a pressure bandage. She opened her eyes and kissed him in gratitude; but no, it was not a sweet or grateful kiss, it was a lascivious kiss, filled with a viper-like tongue, and he tasted blood and venom. He pulled away and Bettina screamed, "You swallowed my Virginia Slim!"

That woke him. There they were again, the statistics; but thankfully the wall clock, based on Greenwich mean time, told him it was time to go home—oh, no, not home! He had to meet *her* outside and go to see "Oh! Calcutta!" Well, at least the Eden Theatre, where it was playing, was in the East Village, close to home. He picked up the phone and dialed home once more. Juanna Donna's breathless question whistled in his ear.

"Did it work? I knew it would! We was all released right away. You hurry home now. We waiting for you. We celebrate your freedom, yo! Land of free, home of bravo!"

Serge told Juanna Donna he had an assignment. Bettina would not take no for an answer. But he'd be there as soon as the play was over. He promised.

Bettina was in a kittenish mood when he got in her limo. She held out a Martini to him—there was a bar in the car—and he took it from her and sipped it until she plunged her long red fingernails into it—God knows where they had been—to retrieve the olive. Then he could no longer touch it. She snuggled close to him and he fell asleep and then she shook him and he woke up. They were outside the theatre. She took his hand and led him into the theatre, led him to their seats, sat him down beside her and seized his arm in both of hers, cuddling it. "Poor little dickey-bird," she whispered, "you must be exhausted."

He nodded, his eyes closed beneath his office stickum spectacles. She said, "I want you to pay attention to this play. I want you to review it." He opened his eyes to a large group of naked actors and actresses prancing about on stage.

"I want you to review their bodies—do a John Simon on them, every crack and dimple—every stretch mark and wimple. If you look closely," Bettina went on, "you can see that every one of them has different colored pubic hair. I want you to match the color of the pubic hair to the particular actor or actress. It's a concept I thought of coming down in the car. Brilliant, isn't it?"

If the Martini was soporific the revue was even more so. Sophomoric and soporific, like wordless naked Shakespeare without the desperately needed poison to put an end to the whole show.

"What are you going to say about it?" Bettina wanted to know, leading him back to the car.

"It's definitely a new concept, a kind of nudist camp version of a Mickey Rooney movie where he shouts out, 'Let's put on a show.'"

"That's not the kind of thing I want," said

Bettina, frowning. "What's the matter with you, Bering-Strait, don't naked bodies turn you on? Aren't you normal? I expected to finally get a little action out of you. Didn't the naked bums of those actresses turn you on?" In the limo she grabbed his crotch. "Isn't anything going on down there? Here, feel this," and she put his hand on her breast. "What about that, hah? I get more erection out of my nipples than you do out of your willy. Doesn't that dickey-bird ever spread his wings?"

"I don't have flat feet," Serge said, inspired.

"What are you talking about?"

"Prepare yourself for a new concept," he said, pulling his hand away, "the shrink at the Induction Center said I was gay."

"Gay? A Nancy boy?"

"Gay!"

"You're not!"

"I am!"

"Well, Sir Gay, Lord Doily Carte," she said, lighting a Virginia Slim, "no wonder I can't do anything with you. Why didn't you tell me that before? Here I was thinking that I was unattractive to you. How could you let me think such a thing? Everybody wants to get into *my* knickers."

"And I would too, if it weren't for the fact that I'm gay."

"Well, now I understand—and I needn't be hurt, need I? Sex and the Single Girl, and all that."

"Not at all," said Serge. "It has nothing to do with you."

"But didn't I see you eyeing Amanda Quaint at the Lunar Society shindig?"

Serge saw that he must be very careful here. What's a sycophant to do? Of course he realized that he was betraying everything Resurgius stood for, but he had already been certified not only gay, but a coward by the government. Why not make use of it? He could still feel the psychiatrist's stamp upon his forehead. "You saw an exchange of—ideas—of concepts."

"Concepts! Of course! You were having an exchange of concepts."

"You hit the nail on the head, Bettina."

"Don't I always, Bering-Strait. I've got big hair up here and I've got big hair down there, and everybody knows it."

"You said it."

"Of course I did, and I'll say it again."

Serge had been looking straight ahead; now he peeked sideways so that he could see what he knew he would see, the Virginia Slim rowing the air as Bettina Battle repeated, "I've got big hair up here and I've got big hair down there. Now, did you match up the pubic hair with the actors?"

"You bet I did," he said. "I wouldn't let a concept like that pass me by."

"You gay guys are so good at such things, so sensitive," Bettina said, satisfied as a cat who has just ingested a goldfish. Something was going on in the cartoon balloon above Bettina Battle's head, an inspiration, a change of plans. She told the driver, "Take us to Studio 69."

Even Serge had heard of Studio 69. It was famous for famous people, for drugs, Roman orgies, and costumed lunacy. It was reported that the psychedelic lighting—swooping, parti-colored Strobes—and ear-splitting decibels were enough to make one drunk as a dancing bear. People who hadn't had a drink or taken a drug staggered out of the place to their limos.

"My sweet little Sir Gay, I forgive you for your coldness, now that I know you're gay," said Bettina Battle, "and I'm going to take you to a place I know you'll enjoy."

"But I have to go home and work on that article about the UNIVAC machines, and I'm already exhausted. I had to get up very early this morning to be at the Induction Center at five-thirty. I shouldn't even have gone to the play tonight. You're running me ragged."

"Nonsense! You're only a snot-nosed kid. Look at me. I'm thirty . . . I'm almost thirty. Besides, I can get you something at Studio 69

that'll keep you awake all night and all day tomorrow, too, better than a rubber thumb up
your arse—if you thought that was exciting.
How do you think I do it? Where do you think
I get my energy?"

"Red diablos?"

"You mean those little candy coated Ben-
zedrine pills? Kid stuff, Bering-Strait! I'm
talking about speed or coke. How do you think
I keep my figure? I haven't eaten since Whitsun."

"What's Whitsun?"

"It's fifty days before the Late Spring
Bank Holiday."

"I thought it was religious—something to
do with Easter."

"Not any more. It's a new concept."

She told the driver to let them out at the
entrance to Studio 69 and drive around the
block until they reappeared. She stepped to the
front of a queue that vanished in the perspective
of the street lights. A zoo of angry voices
jeered them as they were allowed immediate
entrance. Bettina had juice.

Temporal aliasing was immediate. The
flashing, parti-colored Strobes made Serge's
stomach feel like a backward-moving wagon
wheel in a classic Western. In addition, the
concussive, gut-punching music made his heart
flutter. He could see—then he couldn't — then

he could. When he could see, it was like seeing stars, exploding stars, exploding in an aurora borealis of colors, and ink-black night befell his every other augenblick. It was hallucinatory. Bettina said, "Isn't this just heavenly?"

Serge thought it was like being in hell. "It's the pits!" he said.

"Yes," Bettina cried over the musical blast, "it is wonderful."

The ability to hear came and went like the ability to see. She dragged him through the crowd. Familiar faces, famous faces, appeared suddenly before him, then vanished in the ubiquitous chaos of the place. He saw a former First Lady, a movie star, a Wheaties-box athlete, a famously gay writer, and the great, high-cutting unisex designer, Hevonshe. Everyone seemed to be squirming, like worms dancing on their tails, like snakes in their mating ritual. Some wore masks, some wore capes, some were stark naked, and some looked like they were nine days in the pot. Mysterious hands grabbed at parts of his body. Naughty parts and imitation naughty parts, hot and cold, seemed afloat in the air; if you could call the alien-smelling atmosphere, which, if it had a color, would be dark green, air. Serge realized, now, that he was staggering, falling into people, dis-tastefully touching naked flesh and apologizing for it, while at the same time realizing that in

Studio 69 no apology was necessary. That's what they were all here for, grab-ass.

In a flash, he saw Bettina, almost completely naked, handing him a shimmering drink of God-knew-what. "Find yourself a boyfriend," she cried, "you little fairy. This place isn't called Studio 69 for nothing."

And, in another flash, she was gone. But he had spotted something interesting, something recognizable, something that seemed to be alone in a distant corner. With strenuous effort, he achieved the distance between himself and the object of his interest. After all, he told himself, I *am* a journalist. Curiosity is my bag. He got up close and tried to see what he had seen from a distance. The strobes made it difficult, so he found their rhythm and tried to blink along with them, putting together an image in time, a monument.

Yes, it was he—it! What he had read referred to once as "the white mole of Studio 69." The famous artist of multiple images, the former First Lady back there in the crowd being one of them. Yes, there was the old crazy white mop on top, wild and dry as if it had been hung over a clothesline in the sun. It stared out from behind not dark but black glasses. Could it see or did it care to see? Did it need to see? The white mole of Studio 69 sat at a table on a raised platform, so Serge thought that it must be looking out at the crowd. Serge climbed the steps to the platform and stood behind it. Nobody seemed to notice or to care. Oh, said Serge to himself, this is too good to be true. The white mole of Studio 69 was eating from a bowl of Campbell's Alphabet Soup. Serge leaned down and put his mouth close to the white mop and said, "Why Campbell's soup?"

The artist's head did not turn. The artist showed no surprise. He seemed scarcely alive. But a soft voice came in answer to Serge's question:

"Because it's cheap. Now buzz off."

Someone took Serge's arm and led him down from the platform. He looked back to catch another glimpse of the famous artist, but, as in a magic trick, the artist had vanished.

Advised by glaze-eyed guides, Serge went hunting for Bettina through the labyrinthine upper regions of Studio 69. He listened for her British accent as he walked dark halls and light and peeked into large rooms and small. The sweet burning, woody smell of marijuana permeated the air and gave him a giggling contact high, lending to the unreality of the hallways. Other odors assailed his nostrils, animal and chemical, and every light in the place, even the merest hallway bulb, blinked on and off in a heartbeat rhythm, causing his eyes to roll in his head and cross behind his spectacles.

Finally, he found Bettina Battle engaged in a very peculiar activity with a man with devil's horns and a woman with a swishing, camelopard's tail. He waited, half blinded, half drugged, respectfully outside the door, until Bettina's final scream suggested satiation, then stepped in and told her that, if he were to write tonight, he must leave, must go home and go to work, as he was already thoroughly exhausted. How much of what he said registered with her, he couldn't tell—the lights, the darknesses, the concussive music, the man with the horns and the woman with the tail, who knew if his words reached what was left of Bettina's mind? But apparently she had heard something of what he'd said, or understood his body language; and somehow got the message. She gave him a packet of white powder, a silver straw, and told him to snort it up his nose, "Make five lines of it and snort it up your nose," she said.

"You'll be able to work all night and feel fresh in the morning. Time it," she yelled, above the ear-splitting boom-box of the place. "Spread it out." And she waved him away, returning the valves of her attention to the horny-headed man and the tail-snapping woman. He pushed the package back at her and she finally received it, shaking her head in disgust at him, but the lights flashed out, and he could not see what happened next.

Outside, cabs, as well as dark limos, patrolled the real world.

*

At home, Old Glory flew upside down at the top of the mast, figuratively speaking, because they had beaten the draft and raised hell at the Induction Center. There was the sense of a crowd forming for a triumphal march. Government had been bested and, in Serge's case, humiliated. Dagmar Bering-Strait was, for once, not furious; she was, in fact, ecstatic; but she had been furious earlier in the day, as she hastened to tell Serge.

"I tried to bite a cop's ear off, but all I got was a mouthful of blue fuzz from his uniform. Disgusting stuff with the distinct flavor of authority."

Auntie Hoover said, "She had to rinse her mouth out and I still had to pick pieces of government shoddy from her tongue. They were going to charge her with assault—"

"I was furious!"

"—when it was clearly we who were assaulted."

"Don't you ladies want to know how Serge got away?" asked Juanna Donna. "You did what I told you to do, didn't you, niño? You came on strong and feminine like Juanna Donna herself would have done."

"Arms akimbo," said Serge.

"And they just let you go?" asked his mother.

"No fuss—they just let me go. They didn't want me. Gays are undesirables in this man's army."

"We're all so proud of you," said Auntie Hoover.

The three aunties of Boadicea Press applauded.

After a ceremonial burning of his draft card, Juanna Donna led an exhausted Serge up to his bedroom.

"I'm pooped," said Serge, and threw himself on his cot in a short Moog heave of compressing springs. "Thank God tomorrow's Saturday and I can sleep late!" he said.

"Juanna Donna has thought you would be like this, but now is time for work. You don't use it, you loose it! You got to get this story out of you system, or you will be one miserable niño tomorrow. I know you. Now get up and hit those keys. I give you a few diablos to get you going."

As she spoke, Juanna Donna busied herself. She sat Serge up on the edge of his cot, rolled his little typing table with the Olympia over to his knees, and pushed several pillows behind his back.

"I can't, Juanna Donna dear, I'm exhausted. Give me a break." But he didn't want to disappoint her hopes and said, a little weakly, "All right. Get me some coffee and get me some of those little red diablos. Wake me up! Get me going! It's wonderful to have such a great coach who always has my best interest at heart. You are my true mama-papa. Nobody else cares if I fulfill my destiny."

Juanna Donna dumped a pitcher of ice water on his head. "You make me promise, remember?"

"Did you have to do that? I wasn't even asleep!"

"No, but you was trying. Now go get in cold shower and come back and start again."

After a shower and two red diablos, not only did he feel as though he had had a night's sleep, but he felt as if he had more energy than anyone in the world. He felt like Resurgius himself. He could feel the little debilitated straps of his muscles swelling and rippling. Another diablo and he felt mighty, more powerful than a locomotive, faster than a speeding bullet, able to leap tall buildings at a single bound.

"Up, up and away," he cried, sitting down. Wow! He was ready! He had so much to say! A veritable logorrhea was welling up in him, like a pleasant and bottomless regurgitation.

"I feel . . . like Resurgius himself," he cried. "This must be the way he feels all the time. Like a dynamo! I can do it, Juanna Donna!"

"Of course you can, Mighty Mouse. Now hit those keys!" cried Juanna Donna. "Start the next part—go, go, go!"

Pecked raw from before he was a fledgling, and plucked many times thereafter, Serge still had the strength of a raptor whose talons, and even beak, ripped, rat-a-tat, at the torn keys of his Olympia. Oh, he spread his wings wide and soared like a condor over the high Andes of his mind, his telescopic vision seeking out, through his blurred horn-rims, any quiver of the Zorro of justice. In short, his new chapters, imminent and beyond, would even the score.

<u>5</u>

Serge had been up since three the previous morning. The Induction Center seemed like a nightmare from his youth of decades ago, his day at the office a long twilight sleep, "Oh! Calcutta!" was a crazy dream, Studio 69 a walk through hell to get to heaven, his sexual struggle with Bettina Battle—oh my God, he hadn't really married her, had he?—no, that was another part of this multiple act play in which he was starring as a split personality—and his all night wrestling match with his novel—what part of what was that? His head plunked against the Olympia, and Juanna Donna Lorca, like the ministering angel that she was, appeared at his door. She decided that it was time to put him to bed.

"You will finish this Sunday," she said, "and I no mean maybe!" and she tucked him in, kissing his bruised forehead. "What a macho leetle poet," she said, proudly.

He woke at five o'clock on Saturday afternoon with strong feelings of misgiving, but, when he saw the manuscript of *Resurgius* sitting next to his Olympia, he realized that his misgivings were uncalled for—he had not married Bettina Battle, a.k.a Miz Bet, in his novel; he had not made love to Amanda Quaint, a.k.a. Miz Amandalay. What a drooping sadness befell him at that realization! In fact, he had never made love to anyone in his life. Juanna Donna Lorca had once made him a Christmas present of an inflatable rubber lady, but he had never gone near her, because he found her boxed, unfolded personality incompatible with his own, although she did come with a blonde wig, his favorite hair color. Even now she was under his cot, her cellophaned box collecting dust. Yes, as sleep fell away, he recognized himself to be free and virginal, a ripe apple on a branch of the tree of life, an unplucked grape, an . . . oh . . . ripeness is all!

He stepped into the shower and let the water wash the last of his fatigue away, the final dust of that terrible yesterday which he had endured and ultimately triumphed over. For once, he was one up on his hero, Resurgius, who, as he recalled now, had made a botch of things. Serge Bering-Strait had made no botch. Now, as he dried himself, his mind was seized by the image of one person, the beauteous Amanda Quaint. He dressed, knowing that he must see her, that he must see her because . . . because he must tell her, that, when he first saw her, he knew. . . he knew. . . but what was it that he knew? He knew that he loved her, that—it was LOVE AT FIRST SIGHT!

Dressed now, he gathered together the carbon copy of his manuscript and stuffed it into an envelope. He had to share what he had done thus far with Amanda. His compulsion to see her was so powerful that it wasn't until he got off the subway in Brooklyn that he thought of calling her. The whole mindless trip down to Brooklyn to see Amanda was like the tropism of the moth to the flame; but "I can't just pop in," he realized, dropping a dime in a public telephone slot, his heart pounding so loudly that he feared not hearing the dial tone. Oh magic! It was the voice of an angel, his special angel, but what to say?

"_______"

"I hear you breathing," she said.

"It is I," he blurted out. "It is I, Serge Bering-Strait."

"How wonderful! Well, if this isn't the strangest thing. I've been sitting here, curled up on my couch, reading your poetry—

> Now what kind of moon is it, darling,
>   that, so blandly turning blue,
> overhangs us here in greenly summer
>   Brooklyn
>   while the astronauts go round
> and the sea at Coney rises,
> all its little lucky ripples
>   wiping off the darkened sand?

'O Popular Moon!' I just love it! You have a truly romantic soul and should never be required to write articles for silly women's magazines. I wish you were right here with me now."

"Well, I am . . . almost . . . right there with you. I mean, I'm down at the corner telephone booth."

"Well, come on up here right away. I'm all by myself and there's no one I'd rather see. No one! No, wait! Let me finish reciting 'O Popular Moon!'

> Now what kind of moon *is* this,
>   questing for the old romance?

Acknowledging our loneliness,
  we know better than to ask,
returning from the Goldman Band
  and kinder songs of long ago.

Your pearl, your blue, your golden
    loneliness
  bring in our need,
which we acknowledge, seeing you
    sailing light, O, all unburdened.
Burdened by my loneliness,
    I hold her gentle hand in Prospect Park,
    walking from the Goldman Band
  and the dismantling of the instruments.

"And the dismantling of the instruments! You mean the scientific dismantling of romance, don't you? You mean that the symbolic-romantic moon is being taken away from us—the populace—and with it the kinder songs of long ago; but you also mean what you wrote in that poem in the subway, 'The Naked Truth,' that even love is true, if we should make it so. In other words," she rushed on, "it's up to us, what kind of world we live in, whether we listen to 'Lady Be Good,' which I am playing right now, or acid rock—am I right?"

"I guess so," said Serge. "I don't really think about it that much. I wish I had thought to bring you flowers," he added.

"But I have your flowers," she said. "Your poems! A whole book of them. After I read 'The Naked Truth' in the subway, I went right out and bought a copy of *The Last Romantic: Poems by S. Bering-Strait,* published by Boadicea Press."

"My aunties published it as a birthday present to me when I was eighteen. I don't think they liked the book much, though. They're not very romantic."

Amanda Quaint's residence was an ancient Brooklyn Heights mansion on Columbia Heights that overlooked the harbor. The Esplanade was at her back door, where an evening promenade of lovers and loners walked to see the early evening Manhattan lights go on like tuneful notes. Neither could they fail to see the giant hot dog in the sky that refused, night and day, to let them forget, for an instant, QUAINT WIENERS. To some it was becoming an annoyance, to others something like a Christmas tree. The sky over New York was prettier for it, or the sky over New York was becoming junky, it depended upon the subjective aesthetic values of those who looked at it.

Amanda's mansion on Columbia Heights was an inheritance, its twenty-odd rooms too much and too many for one person to feel cozy in. Amanda had set up an apartment on the first floor and left the rest of the house to webbing mites and spiders. She also owned a beach house in Easthampton. Her family's main abode was a five-story brownstone in the East 80's.

She was from a very wealthy family. Her grandfather, Manny Quaint, a billionaire, was known as the Wiener King and had taught her a strong work ethic, along with other old-fashioned values. Now she busied herself, preparing for her visitor—her "gentleman caller," as she quaintly allowed herself to think of him. She loved *The Glass Menagerie.* She put on a pink silk hostess robe and brushed her hair out. She could have been a model, but preferred being a writer. She loved writing and writers and, for her, the best writers were poets. And here she had one buzzing at her door!

He was unprepossessing, a small young man with a baby face and pale red hair, but it was not his physical attributes that interested her. It was the soul of a poet inside of him that drew her to him. She took his wrinkled London Fog and seated him on her couch.

"I'm so sorry just to pop in on you like this," he said. "Lady Be Good" was playing in the background somewhere, Sinatra imploring.

> *Oh sweet and lovely,*
> *Lady be good,*
> *Oh lady be good to me.*

"It's hard to explain," said Serge. "I dreamed about you all night and when I woke up, I had an uncontrollable desire to let you see the manuscript; even though I haven't finished it. I know I told you I'd show it to you when it was done, but I couldn't wait. I had to know what you'd think of it. Maybe you can give me some advice about the ending."

He pushed the envelope containing the manuscript into her hands. "There's a character in it that I think was subconsciously inspired by you—a very beautiful, a very wonderful girl, I assure you—and I was up all night writing about her, and I slept all day, and dreamt about you, and, when I woke up, I felt that I just had to see you. I was on the subway before I knew what was happening. Then I realized that I should call you . . . and why would I think a person like you would be home and free on a Saturday night? I don't know what I was thinking!"

"*A person like me*—what kind of person do you think I am?" She put a silver ice bucket with a bottle of Dom Pérignon in it on the coffee table, two stemmed glasses, and said, "Will you do the honors? Exactly six and a half twists will do the trick."

"I know," said Serge, struggling to open the bottle, "I watch the French Chef, too."

"Of course you do," said Amanda, tou-sling his hair. "I love curly hair. You look just the way a poet should look." Amanda Quaint lit a long cigarette and watched as Serge popped the cork and poured them each a glass of Champagne.

"To your story," she toasted. "I can't tell you how delighted I am to see you," she said, fairly bubbling.

I am so awf'lly misunderstood,
So lady be good, to me.

"Do you like 'Lady Be Good'? I thought you would. It's one of those *kinder songs of long ago* that you write about in 'O Popular Moon!'."

"I sort of . . ." he began, hesitantly—"at the party at Hettie Freed's, the first time we met, I . . . I felt, instinctively, you might say, that you were different . . ."

"Different?" She held her glass at eye-level and gave him a quizzical look.

"I know you're one of them—"

"One of what?" She was frowning now, a slight darkening.

"Well, you have to be . . ."

"Be what?" There was a touch of annoy-ance in her voice this time.

"Well," he said, "you're a writer, an edi-tor. You have to be . . . aggressive!"

Oh, please have some pity.
I'm all alone in this big city.

"As a modern woman, I have to be . . . assertive. But that doesn't mean that every fiber in me isn't female."

"Bettina Battle is female," he blurted, "but you're not like her."

"She's a horrid woman," said Amanda Quaint. "This book you're writing—is Bettina Battle in it? I mean, a character based on her? It's about time somebody did a job on that virago!"

"Well—it's sort of inspired by Plutarch's *Parallel Lives*. It's also sort of a science fiction story, I suppose. Sort of a combination of both. In my life, you see, genres and genders are all mixed up."

"What did you say it was called?"

"Resurgius. I made that up to sound Latin. He's the hero. He's sort of me with muscles."

"You wouldn't be the same with muscles. I'm not attracted to muscle men. I'm attracted to soulful men. Am I really in it?"

"You're the heroine."

"Really! I'm so honored."

"At the end, you and Resurgius get married and live happily ever after. At least, I think that's the way it's going to end. That's the way I'd like it to end."

"I think I'd like it to end that way, too."

The envelope containing *Resurgius* sat on the coffee table.

"Now let me read what you've written so far," she said, assuming an editorial air. "I'm going to take it to my room. You wait here. I'll be back in no time. Play some records. Drink some more Champagne." And off she went, envelope in hand.

In her room, she threw herself on the bed, and began to read.

CHAPTER ONE
THE UPRISING OF THE DONGS

Miz Mandalay, a magnificent Amazon in her early twenties with splendidly developed anti-sex objects, held a dominatrix degree from the University of Xantippe, where she had written an eyebrow-raising thesis in which she had attempted to show that certain ancient Dongs, despite their sexual swinishness, had manifested indications of emerging mental capacity, and had even been capable—this is what had shocked the whole Univacual Council—of a kind of tenderness. Her thesis was later published on Say-screen. Had the times not become more liberal, this thesis might have consigned Miz Mandalay to the lower levels of government.

But these were turbulent times. Dongs were cracking the information barrier, seeking a newer world, protesting the mandate of Shame-school, speaking boldly out from their hiding places, demanding Dong suffrage and all sorts of outrageous rights. Perhaps the most threatening of these revolutionary Dongs was a Spartacus-like character who was often called Resurgius, known for his striking Tarzan-like physique, poetic speech, and wildly flirtatious nature. Lately, he had been in the news several times for acts of rebellion that had landed him in Remedial Shame-school, and no one knew what new outrage this caped crusader with the big R shield on his powerful pectorals would commit next.

Whereas, after the Great Succession, the Dongs were content to be allowed to walk in the gutters, with their heads hanging, and manifesting upon demand every sign of shame, from reddening cheeks to the squeezing of the legs together; today some dared to go about right on the sidewalks. Some even mingled with the Mize—one infamous Dong reportedly was having a lap-dog affair with a superdooper-modelmiz. This, despite the fact that Dongs were not generally allowed to get close enough to Mize to play at lap-doggie, with their tails wagging.

Of late, small, radical groups of Dongs

had been making open protest; as has been said, some had gone so far as to ask for suffrage! (Not that the vote meant anything, even to the Mize; but the idea!)

To liberals of Miz Mandalay's persuasion, these indications of unrest among the once shamefaced Dong population were healthy signs, showing that today's was a healthy, vital society. Some radicals, like Miz Mandalay herself, would give the Dongs a half-vote. She, being a Univacual Council member, knew that the vote was merely symbolic, but also knew that that was precisely what made it important. She would liken it to a valve from which to release the steam of frustration from the pressure-cooker of society.

"After all," she told herself, "the Dongs are human beings, even if they are—well, Dongs."

Ah," sighed Amanda, her heart beating with compassion, and read on. And Serge sat on in terror, waiting, waiting, taking tiny sips of Champagne to wet his dry lips, replaying, over and over, "Lady be Good."

Oh sweet and lovely lady be good . . .

And then Amanda appeared. Her eyes were happy-damp and shined in the soft light of the room. Now she wore a pink negligee that Serge could almost see through to a body that rivaled, if not exceeded, the body of his own literary dream-girl Miz Mandalay. He gulped.

"It's wonderful," she said softly.

"Wonderful? What's wonderful?" Serge said, transfixed.

"*Resurgius*! Your novel," she said with emphasis, seeing that his mind was absent. "I mean, as far as you've gone with it. I really want to know where it's going to go next. Will Resurgius and Miz Mandalay get together?"

Serge had risen to his feet at her entrance. Now she pulled him down beside her on the couch. She put her hand on his neck and felt his fear in the throb of the vein there. Experience told her that he was a virgin and must be treated gently. After all, he was a poet and extremely sensitive. It would be so easy to hurt him and she wanted him so badly now. She must gently, ever so gently, absorb him.

Amanda Quaint leaned over to Serge, framing her face for a kiss. "Well?" she said, widening her violet eyes, and he kissed her, right on her soft red lips. She moved a few inches back, keeping her eyes fixed on his. Her hand was in his lap. "What's that?" she asked.

"Resurgius," he said, flushing.

> *I tell you I'm just a lonesome*
> *babe in the wood,*
> *So lady be good . . . to me . . .*

She drew him to herself and—absorbed him.

In all his twenty-three years nothing so miraculous had ever happened to him. He felt himself enveloped by love, while little estrogens, like microscopic lady-bugs leaping from her, tickled his palm, his chest, his thighs, in a way he might have described in *Resurgius* as heavenly. Oh, oh, oh, this was love. Amanda would have agreed. At last she possessed her beautiful poet, body and soul.

Later, they took a walk on the Esplanade. It was a lovely cool September evening, and many mildly bundled lovers strolled along with them, casting their eyes across the water at Manhattan's blaze of light. They stopped and stared across the harbor, true lovers now, and Serge could not resist reciting a poem he had written at another time when he stood on the Esplanade and looked across the harbor, but that time at the morning lights of Manhattan going dark, a time when he had stood, alone and loveless, and dreamed of having a companion like Amanda beside him to recite it to—

> "When, in the morning remnant of the
>   moon,
> the restless city stirs beneath the stars,
> its buildings hunching in a black tableau
> that forms Prometheus from common
>   themes
> of steel and glass and brick, I walk
>   abroad—

for an hour now—while night lays claim
   on time
for the first time for me tonight (and now
already it surrenders to the sun!)—
I walk abroad requiring only love;
that it may be a morning gift unwrapt
from this dark shapeless parcel and
   received
in utter nakedness; that it be light!
But more than having light, I want to be
one for whom light adventures into
   change,
allowing for my lustings after it
and gives me place to say in certain praise:
O Light, allow me several such days!"

"Oh, yes, 'From the Esplanade!' I read it. It's in *The Last Romantic*. Naturally, I just loved it! I've gone out many times in the morning to see the lights of Manhattan go out like that from here, but, naturally, I could never write it like that. It's just wonderful!"

Serge turned to Amanda. "Are you my girl now?"

She studied his magnified, deeply intensified eyes through his spectacles. "Oh, Serge, I am. I love you."

"I love you too, Amanda."

Amanda's face grew serious. "I've been wanting to tell you all evening—tell you something—and I'm not sure how you're going to like it. I hope it won't make you angry or hurt or anything . . ."

"Nothing you could ever say would make me angry or hurt or anything."

"Well, here goes . . . you may have heard . . . I'm going to be your new boss. Bettina called me this morning to tell me to come in Monday prepared to take charge. She said you were too inexperienced, and told me quite frankly that she didn't want me either but was overruled upstairs. She's lost her influence with the board." She studied Serge. "You won't mind having me for a boss, will you? Of course, that's only at work, you know. Away from work, you shall be Resurgius. I'll see to that."

"I'd heard you were going to be the new editor of *Women's Omnibus.*"

"Bettina Battle is no more. I start Monday. I know you were hoping for the job."

"Bettina's been teasing me with it. But, to tell you the truth, I'm relieved to know that I don't have to give my all for the cause. I could never see myself as the editor of a magazine anyway. As you say, I'm a poet. But maybe I can be of help to you on the job."

"I know you'll be a big help to me, at first; but, eventually, I'm going to let you write what-ever and whenever you feel like writing. You have the soul of a poet and you should do nothing all day but write poetry, and I'll see to it that your little cubicle is undisturbed by mundane matters like food-on-a-stick or UNIVAC III or whatever. You're going to transcend, or I'll know the reason why. I don't even want you to know how I wrested the job from Bettina. Such lovely little ears as yours should be spared the details of the blood sport that is magazine editing. Suffice it to say, blackmail was involved."

"Blackmail?"

"A tape of Bettina being naughty reached the board, I have no idea how."

"Where's Bettina going?"

"She's going to fail upward into politics."

"Oh, thank you, my Jumbly Girl!"

Amanda took his arm and snuggled close, leaned down and kissed the top of his curly head. "My Jumbly Boy," she cooed.

She walked him to the subway, for he had to get home so that he could get up the next morning, Sunday, and work on *Resurgius*. He felt that he was nearing the end, but who knew?

<u>6</u>

Champagne always made Serge hungry and now he discovered that lovemaking with a real woman had the same effect. He was famished, but it was after nine and he didn't want to bother Juanna Donna with his needs. He knew that he need only mention his hunger and Juanna Donna would go to the kitchen and prepare him a hot meal. It would be selfish of him to allow her to do it. So he decided to stop at Schlock's Delicatessen and pick up a chicken salad sandwich and a container of chocolate

106

milk—he was fearless now when it came to chocolate-induced acne; for, after tonight, he must think of himself as a veritable Resurgius, impervious to the minor threats of life. He could almost feel himself turning into bronze.

Now, Schlock's bag in hand, he crossed the street toward Rocky's Rendezvous, peeked in, and saw something shocking. Juanna Donna sat at the bar near the window, in plain view. He had almost passed Rocky's Rendezvous when he realized what he had seen. But Juanna Donna, with a bandage on her nose and a cigar in her mouth, and a bottle of cerveza on the bar before her—she would drink nothing from a bottle, only an appropriate glass—it was impossible!

He took several backward steps to get a second look. What could have happened to her nose that she would need a bandage of such dimensions? She had had only a tiny red spot on her nose, hardly anything at all. Had it become infected? Had she needed the emergency ward at St. Vincent's? Smoking a cigar? Impossible! He entered the bar and stepped up to— *Hector!*

"Hector! What happened to your nose? Why are you wearing women's clothes? Why on earth do you look just like Juanna Donna?"

Hector put a finger to his lips. "Ssshhh," he shushed. "I can get arrested for dressing like this. Sit down and I'll tell you about it."

Serge listened as Hector explained the situation. He told Serge that he had had a nose job with the money Serge had given him. Yes, he knew that Serge meant for him to pay his debt to the loan sharks with that money, but it was not enough, as he soon discovered when he tried to pay an intermediary. The interest rate was so high that he would never be able to pay his debt, over Ten Thousand and going up by the minute. He said he decided that the only thing to do was to become another person—to become Juanna Donna. Well, not really Juanna Donna.

"My new name is Lola Fabiola. The plastic surgeon showed me noses and told me that the one that was best for me was one that looked just like Juanna Donna's because I had the same nose to start with that she had before her operation. What could I do? Then I thought to myself that I should go ahead and make a complete transformation. And here I am, Lola Fabiola, twin sister of Juanna Donna Lorca. We are twins again, thanks to you. And I am safe from the loan sharks. But now I need a job. I can't go back to driving a carriage through Central Park. Not like this. I was thinking of becoming a housekeeper like Juanna Donna. What do you think?"

"I don't know. Wow! You look just like her—except for the cigar. She'd never smoke a cigar, or drink beer out of a bottle. She's too much of a lady."

"Bartender," called Hector Lola Fabiola Lorca, "bring me a glass."

From up the street came the caterwaul of Schlock's untamable burglar alarm, and in the door came a raiding party of badge-waving policemen. In seconds, Serge was lined up with the others along the bar and searched. Fortunately, he had his wallet and identification on him and so was told to leave and warned not to come back to Rocky's Rendezvous. He waited outside to see what became of Hector, a.k.a. Lola Fabiola. Stealthily, the police brought a Black Maria to bear on Rocky's Rendezvous, and, in a few minutes, a half-stripped Lola was being put aboard.

"Get in there, you fag!" cried a cop, and pushed poor Lola roughly through the iron doors.

"What have I ever done to you?" he, she, cried. "Some day we'll fight back," yelled Hector, finally coming out of his closet, becoming the true twin of his sister once again. It was hormone time for Hector—for Lola Fabiola, proud sister of Juanna Donna Lorca.

As the Black Maria pulled away with its sad load of gay citizens, Serge could think of nothing more effective to do than to throw his bag with its chicken salad sandwich and chocolate milk at the retreating vehicle. What would my Resurgius have done, he wondered. Suppose those poor prisoners of love in the Black Maria had been Resurgius' fellow sufferers? How would the great Resurgius have saved them? Serge felt his bronze melting back into weak flesh. He must run and tell Juanna Donna what had happened. She would know what to do. Serge sneaked into the house and crept up to Juanna Donna's room.

Amazed as she was at the story of Hector's transformation and arrest, which Serge blurted every which way he could, like a child telling his mother about his encounter with bullies, Juanna Donna had the presence of mind to call a lawyer.

"Your Auntie Hoover, she una abogada—whats chew say?—she a shyster! Mouthpiece? A *lawyer*, that's it, but I no like to ask her for to help. She likes to get her big nose into everybody's privates. Anyway, she in politics nowadays. Worse than before! And I don't like to use Mr. William Kuntsler, you family lawyer, because everything gets back to them. I'll call Acey Doocy. He understands this kind of problems."

Serge stood by, filled with concern, as she called Counselor Doocy at home and explained the situation to him. Apparently satisfied, she hung up the phone and said to Serge, "Now you no worry 'bout Hector or 'bout me or anything. Everything be fine. Just no breathe no word of this to you mama or you aunties. What they don't knows won't hurt them. Them bodies too busy already."

She handed Serge his manuscript. "I take this from your room cause you Auntie Hoover searches it tonight. She and your mama was furious when they found that inflatable señorita. They take it, but they wasn't half as mad as they be if they read your book."

"Did you read it?"

"Just enough to see what you been up to, you leetle macho, and I know they would not like it, not one leetle bit."

"Why not? What on earth's it got to do with them?"

"Why, it's all 'bout them. And I got to tell you, you make them look pretty funny."

"It's not about them," said Serge, wide-eyed, puzzled, and Juanna Donna could see that he honestly, truly, hadn't realized what he was writing.

"Sergio, you stupido! Anybody can see that it's 'bout them."

"That's not the way a writer works," Serge objected, haughtily. "Sure, I've used a little bit of them, I guess, but each and every character in the story is an amalgam of many people I've met and known over the years."

"Now Serge, how many pipples have you met and know? Except for work, you hardly never go nowhere. You hardly ever *been* anywhere. You stay lock up in your room all the time, like that Boy in the Iron Mask. I'm just warn you, Serge, they ain't gonna like how you show them. The only thing you change is that you made them more real than they are! And, my leetle Negrito, they no see themselves like that."

"Really?" Serge hadn't thought that he was writing realistically but more in the manner of science fiction and fantasy. It occurred to him, not without a certain satisfaction, that he might be more of a Balzac than a Bradbury. It occurred to him that he might be possessed of a strange genius for realism, one of which he was heretofore unaware. A new gravitas weighed upon him, like Earth on the shoulders of Atlas at Rockefeller Center.

"It's past your bedtime," said Juanna Donna. "I mean, if you gonna to write tomorrow and finish that story. Remember, it's Sunday all day tomorrow."

After a night's sleep, Serge woke on Sunday morning, a virgin no more, rolled up his pajama sleeves, and began to write what he thought of as, maybe, the penultimate chapter—

in any case, he felt that he was near the end of the story—of his great Balzacian novel *Resurgius,* the first, as he now saw it, of at least fifty of its kind. It was said that Honoré de Balzac, greatest of all French novelists, drank a hundred cups of coffee a day. When Juanna Donna came bustling in with a pot of coffee, he told her, "Keep it coming!"

<u>7</u>

Serge put the last period to his chapter called "The Eternal Triangle," sat back in his chair, and was considering his work, when Juanna Donna swooshed in, wearing a polka-dot babushka, her pale blue raincoat, and straw-topped platform shoes that displayed her beautiful crimson-painted toenails, and carrying a wet pink parasol.

"I sorry I no keep up with the coffee," she said, breathlessly. "I go to Mass and then I meet Hector and Acey Doocy, the lawyer. I tell you 'bout it later. I know is bad thing to interrupt you when you write, but they wants you downstairs right now. You mama and the aunties have that box with the inflatable señorita in it and I think they pretty peesed-off 'bout it. Look like they have a family council. Bettina Battle down there, too. You better hurry. Here, put on your robe."

"Is it pouring outside?" asked Serge, still in the last scene of his story with Resurgius and his beautiful Miz Amandalay making love.

"It drizzle out, but pour poison down in livingroom. You go down, you walk into hurricane. Be brave, mi poco bravo!" Serge was so involved with his story that he was having a hard time understanding the reality of the habeas corpus or what was required of him. Juanna Donna got him into his bathrobe and pushed him out the door. "Don't tell them I give you that bustious inflatable señorita, or this Spanglish housekeeping he-she never hear the end of it."

Pushed out the door, Serge wondered what a "bustious" inflatable señorita was and how he could possibly be involved with one; but, downstairs, he saw, sitting in the middle of the dining room table, the dusty box with Li'l Abner's naked Daisy Mae on it, gleaming, where angry fingers had clawed the heavy dust away, *bustiously*, through unopened cellophane, and remembered it, of course, his heart sinking, his blood-pressure rising, and his poor, hen-pecked nerves pulsating like Broadway neon.

His mother, Auntie Hoover, Bettina Battle, and Aunties Charlotte, Emily, and Annie, sat at the dining room table and looked up at him as he entered the room as if he were a despicable felon, a disgusting fellow, or maybe they saw him as a mutant—he tried to interpret their gaze. He remembered now that Bettina Battle had become employed as speech writer for his Auntie Hoover in her quest to get Mayor Dimwiddy elected governor; otherwise, he could not account for her presence. Her expression was a bit different from the others, more of a smirk.

"You sent for me?" he asked.

"Don't be too hard on him," said Bettina Battle to Auntie Hoover. "He looks so cute in his little blue robe, like a baby taking his first steps."

"If you please, Bettina," said Auntie Hoover, in the strained, strangling voice of Eleanor Roosevelt, "stay out of this. Now then, as chair, I call this table to order. Is the whole cabinet present? Is the board all here? What is at issue here is the possession of this female-demeaning sex toy. Why was it found in the dark dust-bunnied recesses under your cot? Speak up, Serge!"

"I'M FURIOUS ABOUT THIS!" cried his mother.

His mind only half present—half, back in the brassiere factory hideout of his novel with Resurgius, Serge couldn't help himself: he giggled.

"Do you find this amusing, young man?" asked Auntie Hoover, at first as though from a great distance, but then catching up with reality. Now Serge was here, in the dining room, the box on the table, where he did not wish to be, and no longer snuggling in fiction with Miz Amandalay doing what comes naturally.

"I see nothing whatever a bit amusing about it," cried Auntie Hoover.

The MacGuffin, the dingus, the box, was on the table.

"The Boadicea Press finds nothing amusing about it, either!"

His aunties sounded like the singing group they once had tried to become. Uncanny harmonics! A clangy madrigal!

"It's not a Greek tragedy," said Serge. "I'd forgotten all about it. Somebody gave it to me and I just stuck it back there. I've never touched it. You can clearly see the package is unopened and you can see the dust on it. I should have thrown it away. I just forgot about it."

"I know why you never went near it,"

piped Bettina Battle, in an allusion to her belief that he was gay.

"I won't have such a filthy thing in my house," said his mother. "I don't know what to do with you. You're too old to be spanked."

"Oh no he is not," objected Auntie Hoover. "I'd take the backside of a hairbrush and welt his skinny ass."

His mother continued berating him. "When are you going to grow up? You're twenty-three years old and still living up in that garret, and doing God-knows-what up there. It's a disgrace!"

"I shudder to think," said Auntie Hoover, "what's going on up there while I sleep in my bed at night. I've suspected you of unspeakable acts. I remember hearing you making strange noises. Do you remember? I banged on your door and told you to stop."

"I was fourteen!"

"But did you ever stop?"

"It's the wrong kind of doll," Bettina said. "It ought to be Li'l Abner, not Daisy Mae."

"Shut up, Bettina!" cried Serge. "Nobody should worry about that doll when she's around."

"And just what do you mean by that?" snapped Bettina.

"Yes, whatever do you mean by that?" snapped Auntie Hoover, but Serge's mother put an end to the inquisition by shouting that she was furious, ripping the package open, and shaking the inflatable Daisy Mae out.

"Look at this disgraceful thing!" She held the doll up by its creamy shoulders for all to see and, with a shocking suddenness, the doll inflated, first bustiously, then with an evil hissing sound, its legs lifted to the ceiling, catching the chandelier, and exploding, orgasmically, on a hot, phallic-shaped 60-watter. His mother was left holding an empty, torn rubber skin, and a mop-like blonde wig. Catching her breath, she said, "I want this wicked thing out of my house!"

Bettina Battle screamed with laughter. Auntie Hoover looked at her as if she were missing a cog. The six ink-stained hands of the Boadicea Press were frozen in a defensive position. Auntie Hoover shook her head. "Go to your room, Serge. But you haven't heard the end of this!"

"You aren't the boss of me," Serge said, under his breath, but he ran up to his room in immense relief, even though he knew, tragically, he would never hear the end of it.

Now there was a mad storm outside and long tears of rain streaked Serge's window. "They're all crazy," he told Juanna Donna, who was waiting in his room with a steaming pot of coffee and a box of Danish pastry.

"You no need tell me," said Juanna Donna. "Remember, I work for them before you was born. From the day I come to this house, I lay down the law to them. They run what they want but I run the house. I'm the head honcho, uh honcha, 'round here. I was only a few years older than you now. But I was out on my own too long already to let them treat me how they treat you. I was a servant, but I was *UNE HOMBRE*. Trouble is, they think you a snotty-nosed kid. They don't get it that you a leetle big macho man. You got to assert yourself, leetle negrito."

"But I was never out on my own, like you."

"Me and Hector . . . I mean, Lola Fabiola, we been on our own since we was in short pants. We was on the streets, shining shoes. Tough guys. Plenty macho. Nobody could tell one of us from the other. It was neat. The cops didn't know which one to haul in. In them days, we even use each other's names. Hector would be Juan. I'd be Hector sometime. Then I came out of the closet. I became real me, Juanna Donna Lorca. You *know* twins can't be that different, but Hector, he play macho man, make himself chase muchachas, drinking and smoking like Juan Wayne. Walking around in a closet of his own. But truth catches up—how you say, will out—out of the st*ee*nking closet, as Alfonso Bedoya have said in 'The Treasure of Sierra Madre.' Caramba! What a man! Dios! What big white teeth!

"I met Lola Fabiola and our gay Mick counselor, Acey Doocy, down at Rocky's Rendezvous after Mass, and when I first see Hector I think I am looking in the mirror. And you right, he look just like me again. We twins again! He out of that macho wardrobe, wearing a very smart knockoff Uncle Milty drag gown, a magenta cloche hat with a gold horseshoe pin, turned up for luck, and a feathered boa, despite the trouble he got in last night. Our guy Mister Doocy going to sue the City, Mayor Dimwiddy, and the police department for Rocky's and all the queens was arrested. We got a lot of angry gays down there. I not be surprised if they has a rebellion—a riot even, someday. They'll call it Rocky's Riot, when the queens gives it back to the cops. But, that's all, now. I don't wanna keep you from you writing."

"I don't know if I'm in the mood to write, now—after that brouhaha downstairs. Besides, love has me distracted, too. I'm in love, Juanna Donna."

"I know you are," said Juanna Donna, tears welling in her eyes. "I could tell from the book. It is good thing, to be in love. Tell all about it in you book. Write it all out. Explain it to yourself. I know what it's like. Juanna

Donna has been in love over a thousand times. I have exact number in my diary.”

She sighed, fluttering her long dark damp lashes. “It like you say in that poem of yours that’s riding up and down in the subways, ‘The Naked Truth’— And even love is true. if we should make it so.”

“No, no!” cried Serge. “I was all wrong. Love isn’t willed. It’s a happening. I didn’t know it then, what they mean by ‘falling in love.’ You fall. It just happens. I got that other crap from *The World as Will and Representation.* Schopenhauer.”

“Ain’t he that Kraut philosopher you tell me ’bout? The one whose disgusted mama kick him down the stairs?”

Serge’s eyes went dreamy. He said, “No, you can’t will love. It just happens. You really do *fall* in love. You don’t do it; it happens to you.”

“My leetle niño is grow up,” said Juanna Donna, looking at him with damp, proud eyes, full of motherly pride.

“But don’t you let mama or the aunties see *Resurgius* or they might kick you down the stairs, you leetle Schopenhooser. You know your mama. She’ll be you-know-what!”

“Furious!”

“You better believe it, niño!”

"Does that mean that you don't think the Boadicea Press would publish *Resurgius*?"

"Get real, niño! What you think?"

"But, Juanna Donna, I can't believe that they would refuse to publish a first novel by their own flesh and blood. I just can't believe that."

"I no want to discourage you in any way, bebe. Maybe they not hard as I think they is. The important thing, for leetle Master Bering-Strait, is that he finish the book. We worry 'bout the other later."

"I've got to believe they'll publish it."

"Of course you do, bebe. Don't worry 'bout that now. C'mon, hit those keys! I keep the coffee coming for you—just like—who that Frog writer you been talking 'bout so much lately?—Balls Sack?

"Bal-Zac," corrected Serge.

"Si. Balls Sack!"

At nine o'clock Monday morning, when Serge arrived at his cubicle, he found a memo from Amanda Quaint on his Selectric. The memo was a summons to her office, which had been Bettina Battle's. In fact, he could see through the glass walls of the editor's office that both women were there, Amanda's Ferragamo boots on the editor's desk, Bettina's ice pick heels chopping a circle around Amanda. It was clear, even at a distance, that they were in discord. Bettina's Virginia Slim was dancing between her lips as she spoke. Amanda's arms were up behind her head in a manner indicating glacial unconcern. Serge knocked at the door. Bettina strode over and pulled it open, her cigarette still fanning the air, making warlike smoke signals.

"What do *you* want, you great sexless little twit?" spat Bettina Battle.

"I sent for him, you abusive bitch, and don't talk to him like that," said Amanda Quaint, one eyebrow lifting like a feather on fire.

"Well," said Bettina Battle, "now that you're here, maybe you can help me talk some sense into this woman. I'm trying to turn over the helm to her, show her what to do and how to do it, and she won't listen to a word I say. She comes in here and puts her boots up on the desk and won't pay any attention to me."

"Oh, Bettina," said Amanda, not unamiably, "put a sock in it. Serge, I just wanted to tell you that I re-read your manuscript and I'm even more impressed. That's the project that I want you to devote yourself to all day today. Got it?"

"What is that?" asked Bettina. "What project? I already gave him his assignment. He's on UNIVAC III."

"This is something else," said Amanda. "Much more important." She put her index and thumb together and threw Serge a wink. "I didn't want you to sit all day wasting your valuable time on worthless nonsense, without telling you again how much I loved what you are working on, and that you should carry on with it today." She gently waved her hand in dismissal. "Off you go," she said. "I hope you'll have something very exciting to show me later."

Serge walked through the bustling office as if on clouds. Vindication was in the air. In his mind, the music of Amanda's voice blocked out the racket of the office machines and prattling voices that he heard on ordinary days, days before Amanda was in charge, days of the "Battle of Britain," the dark days of food-on-a-stick, sky-mirrors, and UNIVAC III. But suddenly those days came rushing back like a mountain flood.

Behind him, the door of the editor's office flew open, giant voices were heard, and Serge and everyone else in the office had their attention called as to a catastrophe.

Amanda Quaint and Bettina Battle struggled in the doorway of the editor's office, Bettina screaming like a banshee and Amanda roaring like a lion. Amanda got Bettina facing out toward what had become an audience, lifted a booted foot, and shoved Bettina out of the office and into the copy pool. Bettina's dangling Virginia Slim dropped to the floor, spreading brimstone cinders. Everyone waited, breathless. What would she do next? Serge's writer's mind, gleeful of disaster, was ashamed to think that this Donnybrook could make a great scene in *Resurgius*. Perhaps he could use it. Oh, the cold heart of the creator!

In high dudgeon for dignity's sake, Bettina looked out over the heads of her audience. Then she stomped on her cigarette, strode to the elevator—somehow, too fast for human eyes to see, she had gathered up her things—and plummeted sixty-nine floors, a fallen magazine goddess. As far as *Woman's Omnibus* was concerned, that was the ignominious end of Bettina Battle.

For Serge, and perhaps for some others, this incident was a joy to see; but he, at least, had probably not seen the end of Bettina. The dark thought occurred to him that she could still make trouble from her new post with Auntie Hoover and the Dimwiddy gubernatorial campaign. But, he told himself, *carpe diem*, seize the day and be happy. Two such gifts as his compliment on *Resurgius* from Amanda and the departure of Bettina do not often occur in one day. He was thrilled. From now on, when he looked up from his work and saw the glass tower of power of the editor's office, he would know a friend was there, and a friend in a tower of power is a friend indeed! And so he put himself to work for his friend, trying to grasp the next part of *Resurgius*, thinking, unaware, through his lunch hour.

It felt like some kind of delayed reaction shock. He began to twitch all over. He could feel his eyes rolling in his head; the madman, the lover, and the overwrought poet. He seized his Selectric and stamped out the word — CHAPTER . . .

He couldn't remember what chapter it should be; he typed on—THE BATTLE OF THE SEXES

He felt it! He was going to write prophesy. Yes, and it was inspired by Plutarch's *Parallel Lives* and Xenophon's *Anabasis* (thought of as an advance) and *Katabasis* (thought of as a retreat). The Mize, led by Jaye Edgahoover with Furius at her side, would advance and the Dongs, under the leadership of Resurgius the Great, would make them retreat.

In an earlier chapter, his Auntie Hoover had become Jaye Edgahoover, Boss of the Universe; his mother, Dagmar, had become her second in command, the truly frightening Furius. He had already written of them as these characters and now, inspired by the office battle between Amanda and Bettina, he saw a greater conflict—and a longer novel. All of this formed in his mind in a flying instant in time, a shooting star.

What he was about to write, what he was

writing, this long war, would take up the whole middle of his great novel, *Resurgius*. The novel was going to be a full-third longer than he had originally planned. He was not near the end at all. He was just getting started. Where had his mind been? Of course there had to be the Battle of the Sexes. How not? Onward! Anabasis! Onward to katabasis, the humiliating defeat of Jaye Edgahoover and Furius, and the glorious triumph of Resurgius! He wrote on . . .

The Ovary Office of the Pink House was a-bustle with activity.

When word was brought back to the Emergency Session of the Univacual Council, that Miz Mandalay had been kidnapped by three Dongs disguised as superdupermodelmize, and that she had been taken away in a golden condom-like balloon, resembling a giant wiener, the members of the Council chorus cried for revenge. This was very much to Jaye Edgahoova's taste, and she made good use of all this feline fury.

"Hear me, Mize," she roared, "the Dongs have stolen from amongst us the flower of our regime, the magnificent Miz Mandalay, whom we all know and love. Who knows if right now she is being tortured with Dong love by that musclebound scoundrel Resurgius? First it was our adored Miz Bet who vanished pneu-

matically down a tube. Now it's Miz Mandalay. Who will be next? This is war! And I declare it right now on the Dongs!"

"Yea! Yea! Yea!" came the waves of approval. Vox populi, vox dei!

"Long live liberty!"

"Crush the Dongs underfoot!"

"Stab them with your stiletto heels!"

"Put their donkey eyes out!"

"Hang them by their willies!"

"Freedom now!"

"Then let us withdraw, at this moment of crisis, my Atalantamize, my beloved Amazonian angels, to contemplate the grave implications of our actions and to make detailed plans of attack."

A crescendo of approval!

"It has been your decision," cried Jaye Edgahoova, flushed with success, "I am only your servant." With which she withdrew. The trembling, quaking, expanding Universe was waiting to see what little ole she would do next. Sturm und Drang on the march.

In the Ovary Office, she called for her chief of Shrike Police, one Furius, a flame-haired ex-barmiz from Hoboken, who was notorious for having bitten off the ears of at least twenty Dongs—it was a dastardly lie that she had bitten off anything else or more than she could chew.

"Furius," said Edgahoova, "you are now looking at the absolute Boss of the Universe. The Dongs have played right into my hands. I can wage open war upon them and get rid of Miz Mandalay at the same time. Get me a Pink Dongly. I'm thirsty."

She took out a cigar, a Dongatella, bit off the tip, and began to puff illegally in a no-puffing zone. Authority says yes to itself and no to everyone else.

Other employees went out to lunch or ate at their desks. Visitors came and went, murmuring approval of the new editor as they passed his cubicle. But Serge was heedless of the advancing day until his phone rang and he heard the meek voice of one of his Boadicea aunties on the line—Annie, the one who had always been most sympathetic to Serge but, as he believed, was too afraid of the others to show it.

"Yes, Auntie Annie?"

"Serge, dear, you must come home now, immediately. We're having a family conference about your book."

"What? How did you get my book?"

"Well, your Auntie Hoover was looking through your room and came upon her name, or a name that was *like* her own, on a page in your wastepaper basket. Then she made a really thorough search in your room to find the manuscript it came from and could not. However, it occurred to her that it might be in Juanna Donna's room, and she searched there, and found it, among Juanna Donna's flounces. This was just after you left for work. We've all been reading it ever since."

"Did you like it? Did you think it was funny? Did you think it was realistic?"

"Well, Serge, dear, I, personally, thought it was rather amusing, but I'm not so sure your mother and your Auntie Hoover share my opinion."

"Juanna Donna told me that they might not like it, but I've always been absolutely confident that you and Boadicea Press would want to publish it. Am I right? Is that what the meeting is about? Do you want me to come all the way home just to tell me that you are going to publish my book? Can't you tell me now?"

"Well, Serge, it's not my place to tell you what's going on here," she said in a retreating voice. "You'll just have to come home. It's *that* important."

"You always told me that a good editor could tell a good book by the first sentence, Auntie."

"That's true! I would have thrown *Moby Dick* right in the fire after reading 'Call me Ishmael!' But that's beside the point. Suffice it to say, Serge, you must come home right away."

And she clicked off.

High hopes! They're probably throwing me a surprise party, thought Serge. They must have loved *Resurgius.* After all, Amanda did. Now they want to show me their appreciation of my genius. Only one thing concerned him though—now everyone who counted had read his book, but it, as yet, had no ending, no end to its arc, no climax, no denouement. And his deep, considering mind had been working out this problem as he went about his quotidian business or slept. But he must get more black on white as another practical writer, like himself, Guy de Maupassant, had put it, and now, with this interruption, this distraction, how was he to finish? The gossamer structure of his novel's ending, so carefully being constructed in his mind, was being blown apart. He felt a soft vibration of his exquisitely sensitive nervous system as he contemplated this problem—so he set it aside and returned to first and happier thoughts.

Yes, so far, so good. He had written a blockbuster. "From high to low, doth dissolution climb," as Wordsworth, another bookworm, had put it.

He pulled on his London Fog and went back to Amanda's office. "They want me to come home," he told her. "I'm pretty sure they'll publish my book."

"How wonderful!" cried Amanda. "You go ahead home, but you've got to be back here for my inauguration party at five. There'll be Champagne and the works. You wouldn't miss that, would you?"

"Not for a million dollars," he said.

"Off you go then."

It was a hat trick, the third, and final, great gift of the day! Boadicea Press was going to publish *Resurgius*. He had always been sure that Juanna Donna was wrong, that his mother and aunties would love *Resurgius,* once they had gotten over any superficial likeness to themselves—that parallel lives thing—and they would see the humor in it, for they were big-hearted people, not so petty as Juanna Donna believed them to be. They were his family, after all, his nearest and dearest. Blood was thicker than ink, or something like that. They would recognize his Balzacian, Bradbury-like genius—how could they fail to?—and Boadicea Press would be his. He could see a lovely hardbound volume with Boadicea's trademark of the great woman warrior herself on the cover and his name and that of his great hero—*Resurgius*. O joy!

Dashed!

Just inside the front door stood Juanna Donna's shopping cart, filled to the brim with groceries. Something was amiss.

Serge walked into a battlefield that was in the throes of an earthquake. It was as if several strong women stood face to face at God's Great Judgment Seat. Cripes! His mother was furious, Auntie Hoover was roaring, and Juanna Donna was a whirling dervish. The Aunties of Boadicea Press cowered in a group hug.

"I have warn you," cried Juanna Donna, stabbing the air like Zorro with the épée of a long magenta fingernail, her twenty elaborate bracelets clinking, "since I come here twenty-five years ago, that if you ever, ever went into my room snooping, I would leave this house. But never I caught you before," and her voice rose an octave, "but you go into my room to find that manuthing, and Juanna Donna, she never will not *not* keep her word when she say something, so she is leaving this house, and you lazy-assed intellectuals can just learn to cook and clean by yourselves like everybody else. Soon you pipples be up to you ankles in pig shit!"

"You wouldn't leave me," Serge said, horrified, terrified, mystified, a giant tear rolling down each pale cheek. But no one was listening to him.

"Listen here, Juanna Donna," said Auntie Hoover, waving a finger, "I had every right to find out what Serge was writing about me— about all of us. I'm the boss here."

"*I'm* in charge around here," cried Serge's mother, furiously. "This is *my* house."

"Of course I really meant *you*, dear," said Auntie Hoover. "I'm speaking for you."

"Listen ups! This here is Juanna Donna speaking, and, when she say something, she mean what she say. Juanna Donna keep her sacred word. I am leaving this bughouse. I send for my things," and her hand drew dismissal into the air. "Hasta la vista!"

"Where on earth will you go?" said Serge's mother, placatingly.

"I stay with my sister Hector until I get my own place. I going to retire and live like human being instead of prisoner. I have set aside a bundle. Juanna Donna, she no need this aggravation. She only stay for Serge, and now he grown up and got to learn to be un hombre and stand on his own leetle feet. Youse beeches keep him being like a teeny-weenie niño." She showed them how small Serge was by rubbing her thumb and index together.

"I don't like being bullied by a servant. I *never* liked being bullied by a servant!" cried Auntie Hoover. "*I'm* the boss around here!" she added, jabbing a thumb into her chest. Her face was crimson.

"Juanna Donna is always Capitaine of her ship. And Juanna Donna she is not going to lie to you no more. I gotta new ship just waiting for me if I wants to be Capitaine there; a bigger and better ship than this barge!"

The Boadicea aunties were crying. No one in the house could cook. Would they ever eat again?

"You're the cause of all this," said Auntie Hoover turning to Serge. "Go to your room."

"Yes," said Juanna Donna to Serge, "go to your room! I leave you something there, something very important to your future. You can reach me at Hector's." Suddenly, she was gone. Suddenly, impossibly, Juanna Donna was gone.

Serge didn't know which way to turn. Now he was stupefied. "What happened?" he implored of the giant in the sky, his hands up.

Serge's mother said, "Juanna Donna came home from shopping and found us reading your novel."

Auntie Annie said, "She knew immediately that Auntie Hoover had found it in her room and blew up. It was awful. I'm sure she doesn't mean it."

"She'll be back with her tail between her legs," growled Auntie Hoover.

"I don't think so," said Auntie Annie, shaking her head in sadness.

"Why is it all my fault?" begged Serge.

"Because you wrote that disgraceful libel called *Resurgius*," cried Auntie Hoover, "hereinafter," she went on legalistically, "to be known as Exhibit A, or the traitorous Resurgius Papers, insulting every member of this family, making us look like idiots or worse."

Serge turned to Auntie Annie. "Does this mean you're not going to publish my book?" He leaned over the table and, with great stealth, gathered up his dog-eared manuscript.

"I told you to go to your room!" cried Auntie Hoover. "We'll talk about that piece of trash later. Publish it? We'll burn it! Go to your room, I said, you over-aged adolescent!"

"You've made us all furious," said his mother. "Go to your room!"

"Better go," said Aunt Annie.

"Better go," chorused Aunties Charlotte and Emily.

Dizzy with confusion, Serge climbed the stairs up to the top of the house. He had never felt so alone in his life. He was ostracized, defeated. But then—a warm greeting, a hint of hope. On his cot lay his overnight bag, fully packed, along with his trusty Olympia in its closed case. And there was a note in Juanna Donna's scrawl.

Dear Niño,

I have watch you grow up, but I have watch that these womans don't let you grow up. I packed your bag. There's everything you need. This is your chance to make a man of

The roar of argument followed Serge as he left the house, unnoticed, his overnight bag, containing his precious novel, in one hand and his Olympia in the other. He felt just like Thomas Wolfe leaving Asheville. "You can't go home again," he said, sadly quoting the great Tar Heel. He knew now that he had overstayed his welcome by five years. "*De trop, de trop,* wherever I go," he muttered, rags and quotes always at hand. He should have left home when he graduated from NYU, but it had been so easy not to. Perhaps he *was* an emotionally retarded adolescent, as Auntie Hoover had suggested. Perhaps it was time for him to be a real hero, like Resurgius.

The big changeover party at *Women's Omnibus* had already begun when he arrived back at the office. There were balloons and streamers, and over the editor's door was a banner that read, THE QUEEN IS DEAD—LONG LIVE THE QUEEN! AMANDA RULES! Out of the crowd, Amanda materialized. "Come with me," she said, leading him back to the privacy of her office.

"I've left home," he said in a quavering

voice, following her, unwinding like a spring. "I'm going to the YMCA. My mother and my aunties hated *Resurgius*. They said it was about them—it isn't of course; I just used bits of them, I admit it—and that it made them look ridiculous. Of course, I had no such intention. They have misinterpreted everything. And, for the first time in my life I've come to realize that they have nothing but contempt for me. *And Juanna Donna has left us.* I'm alone in the world and I'm losing the structure of my novel. I can't remember what to do. It's horrible!" Withheld tears puffed his face.

"Life is like a minefield," he said, unoriginally, lugubriously, "you almost make it across and then something blows up." And he dropped his overnight bag and Olympia on the floor of her office, in desperate emphasis.

"There, there," Amanda said, pushing back a cowlick of his rusty hair. "Now calm down."

"Oh, Amanda," he cried, "you're so STRONG!"

"Stuff and nonsense!" Amanda told him that she knew all about it. When he asked how, she told him that Juanna Donna had called her, that in fact, she and Juanna Donna had been in communication for some time.

"She waited down at the corner to see if you would leave and called me immediately to tell me that you had. We are both very proud of you. We know that it was a very brave thing on your part to leave that house. Let me say quickly, my darling poet, that *I* was touched by your lovely portrait of me in the book. You made me a bit ditzy at first, but of course, I understand that the story required it, and I find it incomprehensible that your mother and your aunties can't understand the requirements of fiction. The story is perfectly innocent fun."

"But it has its serious side," Serge put in, puffing up a bit.

"But of course! What's important now is that you write the end of it. Juanna Donna and I have a plan. You are going to live with me and Juanna Donna is going to become our housekeeper. She is waiting, even how, at the house. On the front stoop. So don't keep her waiting. Here, take my keys. As Christopher Marlowe wrote, *Come, live with me and be my love and we will all the pleasures prove.*"

"Oh, Amanda," Serge cried, swooningly. "How wonderful!"

"I have to work late tonight," she added, "after the party. The house is huge and empty and I need somebody to clean it up and to take care of us—especially you, and, more especially, until you have fully given birth to *Resurgius*. I know that Juanna Donna always keeps the coffee coming. Now I want you to

take a few days off and finish your novel—
which I think is hilarious."

"Hilarious? But don't you think it has a
lot of . . . mmm, *gravitas*?"

"Oh yes, Sweetheart, at times it's very
heavy."

"Auntie Hoover—who, as you no doubt
know, my love, is a lawyer—says its libelous."

"Oh, phooey! She's just worried about
any impact it might have on Mayor Dimwiddy's gubernatorial campaign. We'll have
the legal department check it out. Your Auntie
Hoover won't be able to do a thing. Now, off
you go!"

"But Auntie Hoover is dangerous. She's
a . . . *Desperada*!"

"Nonsense! In fact, I might as well tell
you this now: I've been thinking of serializing
Resurgius as a spoof in *Women's Omnibus* with
my article 'Have Some Feminists Gone Too
Far?' as a sort of introduction to it. It'll show
the world that there's a new editor in charge,
one with new ideas, new concepts. How do you
like them apples, my darling?"

"AMANDA RULES!" cried Serge.

<u>9</u>

It was almost midnight when Amanda sat down at the kitchen table in her Brooklyn Heights mansion, weary from her long and difficult first day in command of *Women's Omnibus*, but buoyed and full of hope for the new order of things, the life she would share with Serge and Juanna Donna.

"So, I will be Capitaine of this big casa," said Juanna Donna, serving them tea.

"Yes," said Amanda, "you will be Captain at home and I will be Captain at work. We'll have the third floor fitted out for a complete apartment for you, just as we talked about. I would have had it done already, but of course I couldn't know just when you would make up your mind to put our plan into action and I've been so preoccupied with work. Serge and I will take the second floor. We'll leave the upper floors locked up and we'll all enjoy the parlor floor, where we'll party. You'll cook and keep house. And we'll have the whole place cleaned up, painted, etc., so you can have a fresh start. Of course, I wouldn't expect you to try to fix this big place up by yourself. It's too much. I'll get you some help. I've been very neglectful. Just sat around and let it all go to pot."

"Why you not care? You are reech and important and very beautiful, so why you not care?"

"Why don't I have an active social life? Is that what you mean? I work hard and I don't need men. Most of the men I meet I don't care for. My Sergie, of course, is quite different. He's not a man, he's a poet. I am not afraid to say I love him because I am not afraid of anything."

"I worship you, Amanda," said Serge. "You are the Queen of my heart."

Amanda took Serge's hand across the table, squeezed it, and continued. "It's exactly what I told you," said Amanda, speaking to Juanna Donna, "the other day when we met for lunch. The world is a difficult place and poets lift us above it. I promised myself when I was a little girl, that I would never fall in love with anyone but a poet. Oh, maybe a composer . . . but no, I like poets better. And I think Serge is a great poet."

"Juanna Donna is so very happy that a woman like you know what a good boy and high brow her Serge is."

Pride goeth before a fall, Serge cautioned himself. Listening to the two of them, he was becoming embarrassed. Who would have thought this situation could come to be? Only a few hours ago, his back was to the wall, so to speak. When he had arrived at the office, he had no idea what he was going to do next; and then, quite suddenly, everything changed for the better.

He understood now that these two sitting with him had been like guardian angels all along, watching over him, helping him to do his work, planning this very situation. What wonders they were! But he had to go to the bathroom and he could not sit and listen anymore to himself being celebrated. How could he ever live up to such—he hoped they weren't misplaced—high hopes in him? How all this came to be, he wasn't certain; but it was a miracle, wasn't it? And a further miracle was that the whole ending of *Resurgius* suddenly constructed itself in his mind, like a golden castle appearing out of nowhere. He saw again how he had planned it to go. It was there, and then he entered a tunnel and it was gone and now he had emerged from the tunnel and it was there again. The mind is an enchanted thing, as Marianne Moore, who herself had once lived in Brooklyn Heights, put it, an enchanted and enchanting thing!

Serge got up and went to the bathroom, his ears burning. He lifted the seat and stood over the commode in frustration. He had to go but nothing came. He struggled. He strained. Still, he could not pee standing up. He felt the disconnect between his body and his mind. Finally, he surrendered to necessity, lowered the seat, took down his pants, and sat down, disappointed.

"I know he loves you like a mother," Amanda said to Juanna Donna. "And I know you'll take good care of him when I'm not here. I'm going to be very busy with the magazine, especially here at the beginning. He needs you to watch over him."

"I start right away. I want to get Serge back to work on *Resurgius*. I promise him I see him through and Juanna Donna always keep her promises."

"So do I, Juanna Donna," Amanda said, taking Juanna Donna by the hands in a kind of unspoken vow of close friendship. "I mean, I want him to finish *Resurgius* as much as you do."

"'Cause, you see, Miss Amanda," Juanna Donna rolled on, "I was glad when Serge start to write this book. The reason is, to me, that I believe from the beginning that this book would be like—how you say?—*therapy*. I no smarty-pants, Miss Amanda, far from it, but I under-stands pipple, and I believe he explaining how he feel deep down to himself. They not so bad, those women, his mama, his aunties, they're just all about themselves. They never pay any attention to my leetle Serge when he grow up. I see they keep him like a leetle bird in their big red hands and no let him fly. As he grow, they crush his leetle wings. They don't mean to, I don't think. Just—they don't *see* him. And I know that it must be that you *see* him. You know he is a poet—a special person—and a poet is like a bird that must fly."

"Juanna Donna," said Amanda, "you are a true romantic. I think we're going to get along wonderfully."

"My toothsayer told me that we would. She told me what you would be like to leeve with and I even knew what you would look like before we met, from *Resurgius*. I knew you would be beautiful like Meez Amandalay in his book or like Daisy Mae in the box."

"You mean soothsayer, don't you?"

"No, Miss Amanda, I mean *tooth*sayer. She tells fortune by reading your teeth."

"Oh."

*

Bells were ringing. Serge woke hugging a pillow that a dream told him was Amanda; but she had deserted him and the bed several hours earlier, before light broke. The telephone was ringing. He went into the livingroom to answer it and discovered that Juanna Donna, who had slept on the couch—Amanda had only used one floor of the house as an apartment—was gone as well. He wondered how a cup of coffee would materialize and thought of the kitchen, where it had always seemed to come from. The telephone rang again. He picked it up, but whoever had been there was gone. He called Amanda at work who told him that she had not called him. She was busy.

"Don't answer the phone," she said. "I don't want you distracted from your thoughts on *Resurgius*." She hung up, but it was good to hear her sweet voice.

He went to the kitchen. There was a jar of instant coffee on the table with a note, compliments of Amanda, telling him to boil water, pour it in a cup, and put the coffee in it. Stir it, the note informed him. Apparently, Amanda thoroughly understood his domestic incompetence. Next, he underwent a terrible brain-strain that ultimately resulted in a cup of coffee, took the steaming cup to the windows, which were French doors, and looked out, considering, as he slowly came to full consciousness, what a lonely soul he was.

He went out onto the patio. A breath of autumn, winding between his skin and the inside of his striped pajamas, chilled him and rose goose-bumps. Directly below him was the long back yard, beyond that the Esplanade, beyond the Esplanade the blown and choppy waters of the harbor, where the Hudson and East Rivers met, and beyond that the towering Manhattan skyline. He went back inside, made himself a second cup of coffee, and toured the apartment with coffee in hand, wondering where and when and how he was to finish *Resurgius*.

The phone rang again and he picked it up to hear his Auntie Hoover's voice say, "Serge?"

"Don't call me here. I will not answer." He banged the receiver on its cradle.

Juanna Donna had left him a note on the coffee table in front of the couch. She had gone to Bethune Street to get some of her things, and would shop on the way back. Her trip would take a couple of hours. Back to work tomorrow, Juanna Donna told him in the note. She promised that the first thing she would do would be to set up a place for him to write. He would miss no more than a day away from *Resurgius*. It was nearly noon. Sun and shadows crossed the kitchen floor. The universe, if not himself, was on the move.

The doorbell rang. It rang again. He felt a sense of urgency. The bell was impatient. It rang again. Serge went on a quick search of the bedroom for a bathrobe—oh, if only he had Resurgius' costume with the big blue cape he could wrap around himself—could not find his bathrobe, hurried toward the door in his striped pajamas, and pulled it open a crack. Cool air and bright sun bedazzled him. Autumnal leaves. Then he saw a long red limousine with a mustard colored streak along its top parked in front of the house. The red limo was impressive and he saw it before he saw the man standing in front of him. He saw the man's straw skimmer before he saw the man. The man's clear blue eyes looked straight into his.

"I'm Quaint, the Wiener King. Got any beer?" The man wore a mustard-colored suit, a red hot bow-tie, and tan rattan-like shoes. He was about Serge's height and weight. Those were the only resemblances. He had a pleasant but bulldog-like face and there was a huge, ginger, walrus mustache under his sharp nose. His voice sounded as if he were chewing gravel. He must have been eighty years old.

"I say, are you altogether there, son? I repeat, I'm Quaint, Amanda's granddaddy. I stopped by to see her at the office and she told me to come down and take a look at you. She said she's gonna marry you. This was my house before I gave it to Amanda," he added, pushing Serge aside, establishing his authority, and heading for the kitchen.

Serge followed him, leaving the door wide open behind him. "Here's a box of wieners," said the Wiener King, "Quaint Wieners," and he walked into the kitchen and dumped the box on the kitchen table. "Now how about those beers?"

The Wiener King sat down at the table and looked up at Serge. "Son," he said, "one look at you at the front door and I knew something. I'm Quaint and I'm quick. You've got something missing. What do you suppose it is?"

Serge stood looking at the Wiener King, fully aware now of who he was dealing with, but dumbstruck.

"What you're missing, son, is a mustache! A good thick beaver mustache would make a man of you. Look at me! Everybody does! And they do what I damn well tell 'em to do because I've got a voice like a bear and a mustache like a beaver pelt. You need hair on your face. You're smooth as a boy. Hell, you're as smooth as a girl. But I don't hold that against you. I didn't realize what a gruff voice and a big mustache could do until I was nearly thirty. It was just about then that I went into the wiener business, and the bigger my mustache got, the bigger my wieners got. I drink nothing but beer and eat nothing but wieners. This diet has made me disgustingly rich, and kept me slim and healthy. I'm almost ninety years old, you know," he yelled. "I know that's hard for you to believe. Wieners bring optimism and optimism brings optimal health. Now where's that beer that you keep promising me?"

"I don't know if we have any," Serge finally got out.

"Hellfire and brimstone! How can you live without beer? It's the staff of life in a bottle. Wieners are the staff of life themselves, so beer is like a wiener in a bottle." He gave Serge the once-over. "Why is a young man your age still in his pajamas at this hour of the day? Oh, never mind! Did I tell you, I stopped by to see Amanda at her office and she told me to come down and take a look at you. She wants to marry you. You look O.K. to me. Hell, you must be or she wouldn't want you."

"Marry me?"

"Why, yes, of course! What do you think you're doing here? She told me you're some kind of poet. But that's O.K. You won't need money in this family. She makes a lot and I have the rest. The main thing is that you're a good decent chap. But I still say that that baby face needs some hair on it, poet or not."

There was a racket in the hall and five workmen in paint-splashed coveralls walked into the kitchen. One of them said, "We're the painters. You left the door open so we came in. Where do we go? What do we do?"

"Hello boys, I'm the Wiener King," said the Wiener King. "You boys got any beer? When I was a house painter, which I was when I was young, we always brought beer along with us, and nowadays they got those cooler things to keep it chilled. We didn't have them. We had to drink warm beer. I repeat, boys, where's the beer? If you've got the beer, I've got the wieners, as you can see. Had any lunch?"

In ten minutes, five workmen, Serge, and the Wiener King sat around the table, drinking beer and talking, while the aroma of grilled wieners filled the kitchen, the Wiener King re-galing the painters with tales of ancient days when he himself had been a house painter in the Bronx.

"Now let me tell you something that's REALLY interesting," the old man shouted, clearly feeling his beer; but he was stopped by the cling-clang entrance of Juanna Donna and Lola Fabiola, a.k.a. Hector.

"Now let me tell *you* something really interesting," said Juanna Donna. "This party is over! You painter men get upstairs and get busy. Third floor. You know what to do. And make room for movers. They be bring up my things. Serge, you been drinking beer?"

"No, no, Juanna Donna," said Serge, shaking his head, "only coffee." Serge answered the elaborately costumed person who asked him the question because he assumed that only Juanna Donna would ask such a question; but, in all truth, he wasn't sure whether he was speaking to Juanna Donna or Hector, so alike were the twins now. They had become doppelgängers again.

When he first knew them, as a little boy, they were identical; then Juan turned into Juanna Donna, gradually, but before his eyes, and now Hector had turned into Juanna Donna, or Lola Fabiola, and he could hardly tell them apart but for what they said. After a moment or two of sharp contemplation, Serge stretched out an arm and indicated the person he thought was Juanna Donna.

"Mister Quaint, I would like you to meet our housekeeper, Señorita Juanna Donna Lorca, and her bro—eh, sister—Señorita Lola

Fabiola." He scratched his head. Did he get it right?

"Manny Quaint here, Amanda's grand-daddy," yelled the Wiener King. He got to his feet and gave the twins a courtly bow. "I may wonder how many beers I've had, for I'm seeing double. How amazingly charming it is to meet two such attractive señoritas. Nature might have been satisfied with one. Mother nature might have thought that she had pressed her powers to the limit in creating one such beauty, but *two*—two perfect specimens of womanhood—well, it simply takes my breath away. If I had the stamina that I had in youth—say, at seventy—I wouldn't know which one of you to pursue first. But one question might clear my mind. Which one of you likes wieners?"

"Both of us like wieners," said Juanna Donna, taking two from the table and handing one to Lola Fabiola.

"Alas," cried the Wiener King, "I am confounded. If only I were a polygamist and could marry you both, my Spanish beauties."

"Then we would be very rich?" asked Lola Fabiola.

"You would indeed, ladies," yelled the Wiener King, "but there's a law against what I have in mind, even though with enough beer and wieners aboard, it's a fact that I can run in two directions at once. In other words," he said, "I can defy nature itself," and he winked and donned his skimmer. "Serge," he said, "I feel a bit wobbly. See me to the front door, will you?"

Two of Juanna Donna's movers carrying a heavy chest of drawers toward the staircase passed them in the hall.

At the front door, Serge had the wit to ask, "Do I meet with your approval, sir?"

"Oh, you already had my approval when I came. Whatever she wants—well, Amanda always does the right thing, so I know you're the right thing for her. I just wanted to get a look at you, see what it is that she likes about you, that she loves about you, and I think I can see it. I think I see a good heart and a sweet nature. Don't hide your light under a bushel, son. If Amanda loves you, you have a right to be proud. There's a durnblasted good reason for that love. But you need some hair on your face. Grow that mustache!" The Wiener King's chauffeur came up the steps and took him by the arm.

Serge hadn't thought so far as parental approval. "Do you think Amanda's parents–"

"Don't worry about Amanda's parents. I'm the one you have to impress. What I say goes. They're rich from having me; I'm rich from having money. I'm the *law.* *I'M* THE WIENER KING!"

The patient chauffeur helped the Wiener King down to his limo, where the W.K. turned around and yelled, "Later!" And, with one last wave of his skimmer, he was off in his Wienermobile.

The after-image of the Wienermobile had not yet cleared from Serge's mind when Bettina Battle appeared at the foot of the steps as if materialized by a Roddenberry beam. She looked up at Serge. "Who was that?" she called. "Wasn't that the Wiener King?"

"Bettina! What are you doing here?"

"I'm a reluctant emissary from your family. They've had a change of heart. Your Auntie Annie talked to your mother and your mother talked to Auntie Hoover and Auntie Hoover sent me to get you. Why won't you answer the phone? You could have saved me the trip. I had no desire to come down here to Brooklyn. I don't particularly want to see you, after the way you've treated me, and I certainly don't want to run into Amanda. But I am under orders from your Auntie Hoover to bring you home for your mother's sake. She's not furious any more—*au contraire*. Aren't you going to invite me in?"

"All right," said Serge, stepping aside, "if you must; but this is a very busy house today."

A large white van pulled up and parked where the Wienermobile had been. A number of bustling men appeared from its recesses and in seconds were carrying pink bathroom fixtures up the steps, forcing Serge back. Serge heard Juanna Donna directing them up to her apartment. The men brought in a bath and shower unit, a sink, and, following behind the bobbing commode, Bettina Battle entered.

"I've been here before," she said, seizing Serge's hand and pulling him into the kitchen behind her.

The house rang with the hammering of construction, and the workmen who passed through the kitchen did double-takes, seeing Bettina, statuesque and pulchritudinous in her mini-skirt and five-inch heels. Serge saw their eyes pop and knew that their mouths were watering. "Fix me a nice cup of tea," she said, sitting down at the table.

"I get it," said Lola Fabiola through seven veils, innocent of Serge's desire to get Bettina out of the house.

Bettina lit a Virginia Slim and let it dangle from her crimson lips while she talked. "I've been ordered to bring you home," she said, "dead or alive. I just have to get you there and then you can do whatever you want after you've seen them. My job is at stake. Your Auntie Hoover doesn't take no for an answer. I'll lay my cards on the table. How much do you want?"

"Much what?" asked Serge, not getting her drift.

"Money, of course. I'll give you five hundred to come to Bethune Street with me. This is the first important job your Auntie Hoover has given me as her assistant and I've got to get it right. Five hundred bucks isn't bad for a trip to the Village, is it? Look, the money's about two-to-one, so I'll make it five hundred pounds. What do you think?" She took a sip of tea from the cup Lola Fabiola had set before her and blew a tornado of smoke at Serge.

"I wouldn't go back with you if you gave me the Exchequer and threw in Fort Knox. I wouldn't go anywhere with you anyway. I know what you get up to in that damn limousine of yours. And Amanda wouldn't like it either."

"Amanda! Amanda! Do you know what that bitch girlfriend of yours did to me? She blackmailed me! She taped me when she was in my car with me and gave it to the board of directors of *Omnibus*."

"Magazine editing, I've heard, is a blood sport," said Serge. "Amanda told me so."

"Aren't you shocked, Mister Goody Two-Shoes?"

"A woman's got to do what a woman's got to do," said Juanna Donna, appearing in the doorway. Bettina looked at her, whirled about in her chair, and looked at Lola Fabiola.

"My God!" she cried. "There're two of you. I thought the one who got me the tea was Juanna Donna. Who's the other dervish?"

"That is my bro—" started Juanna Donna— "my sister Lola Fabiola. Maybe when you come to Bethune Street you saw my brother Hector. Well, he is my sister, and once again he is my twin. I am glad there are two of us but I am sorry there is even one of you, Mzzzzzz Battle. Why you let her in, Serge?"

"Just one minute here," said Bettina Battle, pulling herself up to face an enemy attack. "Who do you think you're talking to?"

"Juanna Donna know who she is talking to, who is not who she pretend to be. Juanna Donna, she hate a fake, a big tall fake in a miniskirt." She went around the table and lifted Bettina to her feet, stood her on her towering heels.

"You big bony stack of stink," she cried. "Juanna Donna has dream of giving you heave-ho lots of time from Bethune Street but now in Amanda's house, I can do it, because I am Capitaine here."

"Unhand me," cried Bettina, "you walking stack of carnival tents!"

"I unhand you O.K., because I no like to touch you, you phony phooey! I catch you stand up to pee at Bethune Street. You are what Serge call a Dong." She looked at Serge and

Lola Fabiola and pointed at Bettina.

"This is no woman! This is like me and you, Lola, but too phony to be what she is. She got a string on her crotch that she tuck back up. *He* got a string, the beech!"

Now she lifted Bettina Battle and carried her kicking to the front door, Serge and Lola following. "You go back to Auntie Hoover with your tail between your legs and she take care of the rest of you."

"Serge," cried Bettina, "for God's sake, help me!"

Juanna Donna set her—eh, *him*—down on the stoop and closed the door after her—eh, him. A couplet from Edgar Allan Poe popped into Serge's mind—

Is all that I see or seem
But a dream within a dream?

He went to Amanda's bedroom, found his clothes, and got dressed. No one noticed as he left the house. It was good to be out and away from all that hammering and yammering. He spent the afternoon contemplating the sliding slate of the harbor from the Esplanade, watching people promenade, putting the parts of the end of *Resurgius* together in his mind, and watching the sun slide down into the west. And then, not soon enough, it was time for his angel to come home, and he returned to the house. What a relief! The workmen were gone.

Hector—Lola Fabiola—had gone back to Bethune Street. Juanna Donna was making *arroz con pollo*. The house was quiet. Later, after dinner, alone, he told Amanda what had happened with Bettina. "How could I have missed such a thing?" he asked Amanda. She saw that he was in a state of consternation.

"So far as I know," said Amanda, "only Juanna Donna and I knew about it. Look at her. No one else could possibly tell." Amanda told him that Bettina Battle was out of their lives forever. She told him that she had talked to Juanna Donna about what had happened, and that he should not concern himself with it, but concentrate his attention on his finishing *Resurgius.*

There was no question that Amanda knew best, that she was the Captain of him, so he listened to her advice, dreamily snuggled his head into her more than ample bosom, and went to sleep while watching Resurgius, broadsword in hand, slaying a dragon that looked rather a lot like Auntie Hoover.

Waking, alone again, Serge, sandy-eyed, found his way to the bathroom. He stared at himself in the mirror. He needed a shave. He decided not to touch the area under his nose and above his upper lip. Staring hard at his reflection, he thought he could detect the beginning of a bushy red mustache, something that might one day resemble the Wiener King's. But perhaps it was only morning shadow enhanced by his hopeful imagination. He sat down on the john to pee, realized what he was doing, and jumped up. He turned around and lifted the toilet seat and filled the bowl the way Gargantua had filled the Seine, the way Resurgius had filled the River Slime. O joy! O gratification! *Viva machismo!* Hooray for John Wayne!

"Good day, Pilgrim," he said to his willy, shaking the last drops from it, "and thanks."

Serge found a pot of coffee waiting for him in the kitchen, and a note directing him to the second floor, where everything had been prepared for his task of finishing *Resurgius*. He had slept late again, and Juanna Donna had to shop; but she would be right back, her note informed him. Walking about in his P.J.s., Serge began to read his penultimate chapter: "A Byzantine Betrayal."

"O, betrayal!" Resurgius cried, "O, treachery!"

"Alas," said Miz Amandalay, climbing in next to him, "she loved you not too well, but, rather, too wiseguyly."

Wiseguyly! It was as if he had intuited Amanda's knowledge of Bettina's secret. He began to put things together. When Bettina kidnapped—well, commandeered—Amanda from the Lunar Society party, something must have happened. Amanda must have discovered Bettina's secret—and the tape!—she must have recorded everything Bettina said—and he had enough experience with Bettina to imagine what that might have been—and later sent the tape to the board. *Blackmail!* Now he understood clearly. Oh, what a mighty woman was his Amanda Quaint! If only she could share her strength and empower *him*!

Everything had been arranged for him—chair, table, typewriter, and paper. He sat down at his Olympia, and—DA-DOT, DA-DA!—began—CHAPTER . . .

Again, he couldn't remember what chapter it was. He was never any good at numbers.

Losing shame and gaining pride with every advance, the Dongs had fought their way to the Pink House. It was over for the Evil Mize. The rest of the female population sent emissaries to the Dongs to inform them that they, too, were happy to be out from under the oppressive thumbs of the dictatorial Mize. The war was over.

Handy Mandy, as Resurgius sometimes called Miz Mandalay, because she had been so helpful to him during the war, asked Resurgius what he thought should be done now that they were in power.

"The New Order should not be one in which either sex is in a superior position, nor should it be one of equality—male and female are obviously not the same. They are two halves of a whole. In other words, they are complementary." He studied the beautiful woman before him. "Ah, but you are my better half."

He went on: "This revolution business is too much for me," he said, pushing his horn-rimmed glasses up through his lush locks to the top of his extra large and scholarly head. "I just wish I could go off to some distant paradise and lead a quiet, meditative life, reading the rest of the Western canon, re-reading all the wisdom books, and studying Eastern philoso-phy."

You're just too tired," Miz Mandalay soothed. "You've been through hell."

"To hell and back," Resurgius said stoi-cally.

"My hero," Miz Mandalay commented, squeezing his powerful thigh.

"Mandalay?"

"Yes, dear?"

"Would you consider giving up all this— the political life, I mean—and running off with me to a desert planet, where it would just be you

and me and the drifting meteorites?"

"Well, dear, I do so hate to see you give up all that you've fought so hard for; but, naturally, my love, whither thou goest, I will go. In the face of love, the life of politics seems but pale mundane trash. After all, as Jaye Edgahoova might say, politics is nothing but the profound entertainment of the people. I am no longer that interested in entertaining the people. I am in love, and therefore selfish; and perhaps that is the best way to be. At least, if I'm minding my own business, I won't be doing them any harm, poor devils. Pity poor people, they have no sense. I often wonder why they do what we tell them to."

"Because they're afraid to think for themselves. Because they mix us up with their ideals, their hopes and dreams. They're the lemmings and we are the force of the ocean, drawing them to us. That's all."

"It's really quite sad."

"Then you'll go with me?"

"Anywhere, anytime."

"Tomorrow morning, to the moon. From there we can get the shuttle on to Mars."

"It'll be like an old-fashioned honeymoon."

"Let's start tonight. The honeymoon part, I mean."

"Oh, you!"

But it was only a dream, and in dreams begin responsibilities, as the ancient Irish were wont to say. They knew that people, all people, needed them as they represented, as a power couple, the true balancing and partnership of the sexes.

Next day, Resurgius brought charges against Miz Bet and banished her to the dark side of the moon, where rumor had it that she joined Edgahoova.

The disposition of Furius was another matter. The woman was half mad, and so in good conscience could not be punished. Resurgius, after much deep deliberation with Handy Mandy, decided to have her institutionalized in one of those charming new Neptunese padded cellular houses in Washington Square in Greenwich Village.

Resurgius and Handy Mandy were married. Both died in office, Resurgius first—of a heart attack from carrying Handy Mandy's luggage—and Handy Mandy, in her sleep, twenty years later. Both were beloved by the populace.

10

"That last chapter is wonderful," said Juanna Donna. "I so glad for you that you have done it and so proud of you, my little Mighty Mouse. No, no, Juanna Donna has said wrong. You not my little Mighty Mouse. You my mighty macho man, Resurgius himself! I never call you anything but my mighty macho man again, 'cause look what you have done!"

"And Juanna Donna, I have more big news for you. You know my problem . . ."

"You mean the way you has to go to the bathroom?"

"I do it like John Wayne now. I could stand up and do it right against a tree."

"Is a miracle! And you know what do that to you? Is because you wrote this book. And what is that I see beneath your nose? Don't turn away. You don't fool Juanna Donna. Is a leetle red mustache coming out there? Very macho!"

"And I owe it all to you, Juanna Donna. To Amanda, and to you and those little red diablos that kept me going when I was so exhausted at night."

"Phooey! There is no such thing as little red diablo. I have give you Doctor Spinoza's Red Regulators. They for constipation, sluggishness, and change of life—which both of us is going through. See? You stand up at the toilet. They make me sit down. You no think I would give my bambino bad drugs, do you? I never do that!"

"But why did they work? I mean, how did they keep me up to work?"

"They didn't! Is all a state of mind, niño—I mean, Resurgio—all a state of mind. The coffee must have helped, but mostly it was just being encouraged. Encouragement what inspired you."

*

"Well," said Amanda, late that evening, as she and Serge sat together in bed, "I love it!

But, as your editor, I think you're going to have to re-write that whole last chapter.

"No! What's wrong with it? Juanna Donna said it was wonderful."

"Why just everything! Why should you die and I live twenty years more?"

"That's what the actuarial charts tell us. On the average, women live twenty years longer than men. Besides, Miz Amandalay isn't you and Resurgius isn't me. They are rounded, compound characters, each made from several people."

"Nonsense," said Amanda. "It's plain as day who they are. I don't like Handy Mandy, either. That's an awful name."

"But remember, in an earlier chapter, Miz Mandalay tells Resurgius to call her that. She says, 'From now on, I want you to call me Handy Mandy. Miz Mandalay is my old Uni-vacual name'."

"And another thing," said Amanda, ignoring him, "all of these names have to be changed. I can identify everybody in this story. And what's more, I want a more romantic ending."

"Are we having our first argument?"

"Now, don't pout, Serge! Say, what's that under your nose? Are you growing a mustache?"

"Well—"

"Don't worry. I like it. It gives you a certain—*savoir faire*." She took off her reading glasses, put them and the manuscript on the bedside table, and slid an arm around his neck. "Come on, Sweetie Pie, come close."

Next morning, Juanna Donna woke them. "I got message for you," she said, nodding at Serge. "Mama call and wants you come to Bethune Street."

Well, it was here—the moment he had dreaded. He must confront his family and tell them that he was not going to return to them; that he had a new life. But now that *Resurgius* was done, and with his new red mustache on his prow, he felt that he could do it.

On his way to the subway, Serge spotted the Quaint Wiener airship sailing off in the distance over Brooklyn, a red wiener hovering in the blue morning sky. He told himself it was a talisman, that it indicated that his meeting with his mother and his Aunties would not go too badly.

At Bethune Street, the door was opened by—

"Hector!"

"No, no, no, señor Serge! I am proud to be Doña Lola Fabiola Lorca, the true queen of the Lorcas. My sister, Juanna Donna, is only pretender."

"It's amazing," said Serge. "I only just left her and I feel as if I'm seeing her again. It's as if she'd been transported in a time machine."

"Come on in, your mother and your aunties are waiting to see you. Be nice. I think they want to make up with you."

Serge's mother, his Auntie Hoover and the Boadicea triplets were gathered in the living room, as for a family conference. Serge felt as if he had entered a scene from a Victorian novel. Mother and aunties didn't seem to know quite what to say or how to say it.

"It's good to see you all looking well," Serge said. It seemed a bit formal, so he added, "Look, I'm sorry if I caused you any pain. But I'm out on my own now, and I'm going to stay out, and—"

"Oh," said Auntie Hoover, "we don't mind that you've left us . . ."

"No," said his mother, "we're glad to see that you're standing on your own two feet. We never meant to hurt you. After all, you're twenty-three years old and you should be out on your own. My God," she cried, "you've got a whispy whisk-broom under your nose!"

"And maybe," Auntie Hoover rolled on, "we lost track of how old you were because sometimes it seemed as if you were never going to go out on your own. We're not really mad because you left home. But did you have to make such fun of us, ridicule us that way, in that awful book? It was shocking to think that you hated us so much. After all, we're just women, and you were a boy, and maybe we made mistakes bringing you up, but we always loved you."

"We always loved you," echoed his mother.

"We always loved you," chorused the three Boadicea aunties.

"And you made us look like monsters," said Auntie Hoover.

"But the characters in that story weren't *you*," said Serge.

"Jaye Edgahoova?" Auntie Hoover truly wanted to believe Serge but looked doubtful.

"And anyway," said Serge, "I'm a poet who wrote a novel, not a novelist who writes poetry. I should stick to what I'm—well, I write better poetry than I do fiction."

"I should say," said his mother. "The novel made me furious, and I'm so relieved to hear that you really didn't have us in mind."

"We should say," chorused the three aunties. But Aunt Annie threw him a wink.

He couldn't help smiling, and suddenly everybody was smiling, even Lola Fabiola, standing in the doorway with a tray laden with coffee and croissants.

"When can we all meet your Amanda?" asked Auntie Hoover. "Is it true, that she's related to Manny Quaint, the Wiener King?"

"She's his granddaughter."

"I should have Bettina contact him about a campaign contribution," she said. "He's richer than a king."

"And a wonderful old guy," said Serge. "He's going to buy us a slam-bang wedding."

"When's it to be?" asked his mother, full of uncharacteristic, girlish excitement.

"This coming June, of course. Amanda wants to be a June bride."

A comedy—even a sex comedy—thought Serge—should end with a wedding. And in June there was a photograph on the cover of *Women's Omnibus* magazine of the wedding of the Wiener King's granddaughter, Amanda Quaint, and the young poet, Serge Bering-Strait.

The ceremony took place in Central Park, at the Tavern on the Green, where the Quaint Wiener airship had touched down on a day when the sky was blue as only a wedding day sky can be. The photo on the cover of *Women's Omnibus* showed the beautiful bride helping her dashingly mustachioed groom into the gondola of the famous Quaint Wiener airship.

Whatever secret location they sailed off to, their honeymoon would most certainly be in paradise. Yes, Amanda had removed the ring from Serge's nose and put it on his finger, and Serge just knew that, like a prince in a fairy tale, a fairy tale with a beautiful princess, they would live happily ever after.

E.M. Schorb's first novel, *Paradise Square,* received the Grand Prize for Fiction at the Frankfurt Book Fair. His *A Portable Chaos,* followed and was awarded the Eric Hoffer Award First Prize for Fiction. His *Murderer's Day* was awarded the Verna Emery Poetry Prize and published by Purdue University Press. Schorb's *Time and Fevers* was the First Prize recipient of the Writer's Digest International Award for Poetry. It also won the Eric Hoffer Award. *Dates and Dreams: Short Fictions, Prose Poems, Cartoons* won the First Prize for Poetry in the 2016 Writer's Digest International Book Awards.

www.ingramcontent.com/pod-product-compliance
Lightning Source LLC
Chambersburg PA
CBHW050516160726
48003CB00001B/331